V-Kar's Epic

by: ZeRoAl

V-Kar's Epic
A Speaker For The Dead Book
First ebook edition: April 2020
ISBN 978-1-0694331-6-9

Published by OMDN Press
www.omdn.ca/
Manufactured in Canada
10 9 8 7 6 5 4 3 2 1

0 Short Stories For opWorldPeace
 Audio: 978-1-9990271-8-6
 EBook: 978-1-0694334-4-2
 Print: 978-1-997595-00-7
1 Blasphemous Beginnings
 Audio: 978-1-9990271-9-3
 EBook: 978-1-0694334-6-6
 Print: 978-1-997595-01-4
2 RetroGenesis
 Audio: 978-1-0694331-0-7
 EBook: 978-1-0694334-8-0
 Print: 978-1-997595-02-1
3 Another Awakening
 Audio: 978-1-0694331-1-4
 EBook: 978-1-0694334-9-7
 Print: 978-1-997595-03-8
4 Birth Of A Deceiver
 Audio: 978-1-0694331-2-1
 EBook: 978-1-0694334-3-5
 Print: 978-1-997595-04-5
5 Retrograde of Jealousy
 Audio: 978-1-0694331-3-8
 EBook: 978-1-0694334-5-9
 Print: 978-1-997595-05-2
6 Recursion Of Infinities
 Audio: 978-1-0694334-2-8
 EBook: 978-1-0694334-7-3
 Print: 978-1-997595-06-9
7 V-Kar's Epic
 Audio: 978-1-0694331-6-9
 EBook: 978-1-9990271-3-1
 Print: 978-1-997595-07-6
8 The Center Of Time
 Audio: 978-1-0694331-4-5
 EBook: 978-1-9990271-4-8
 Print: 978-1-997595-08-3
9 NyNe's Story
 Audio: 978-1-0694331-5-2
 EBook: 978-1-9990271-6-2
 Print: 978-1-997595-09-0

I dedicate this one to my step father, (who is not) John F Kennedy, all who have suffered under secret societies, and to anyone daring to venture near the center of time - you have been warned..

V-KAR'S EPIC

Chapter 1: The Jungle Roars

The sun burned fiercely over a lush, prehistoric Earth. Towering ferns and cycads swayed in the humid breeze, their emerald leaves glistening with dew. The air was thick with the scent of damp moss and the tang of sap, carried on winds that whistled through canopies high above. The jungle teemed with life: the screech of pterosaurs echoed across the skies, the distant bellow of a triceratops rumbled like thunder, and beneath it all, the ceaseless hum of insects filled the air like a living symphony.

In this wild, untamed world, the predator known as V-Kar prowled.

The Hunt

V-Kar crouched low among the dense underbrush, his scaly hide blending seamlessly with the dappled shadows of the forest floor. His yellow, slit-pupil eyes narrowed as he watched his prey: a lone hadrosaur grazing near a cluster of flowering cycads. The herbivore's beady eyes darted nervously, its nostrils flaring as it sniffed the air.

V-Kar tightened his clawed grip on the vine-covered log beneath him, his tail swaying silently to balance his weight. His heart pounded, but his breaths came slow and deliberate. He had hunted countless times, but this moment - the stillness before the strike - always thrilled him.

The jungle fell silent. Even the insects seemed to hold their breath. Then, with a sudden burst of movement, V-Kar leaped forward, his powerful legs propelling him toward his prey.

V-KAR'S EPIC

The hadrosaur's cry pierced the air as it bolted, its hooves churning the earth into a spray of mud and leaves. V-Kar's claws scraped the ground, his muscles coiling as he surged after the creature. The chase was swift, brutal, and over in moments. With a final lunge, V-Kar sank his fangs into the hadrosaur's neck, its warm blood spattering his snout.

The jungle erupted back into noise: the squawk of startled birds, the rustle of unseen creatures fleeing deeper into the foliage. V-Kar stood over his kill, his chest heaving, his senses sharpening as the tang of blood filled his nostrils.

But his victory was interrupted by a low, guttural growl.

An Interruption

V-Kar turned sharply, his eyes locking onto the massive figure emerging from the jungle. A towering theropod, its jagged teeth bared, stomped toward him with slow, deliberate steps. The ground trembled beneath its weight, and the air grew thick with the sour stench of its breath.

The theropod let out a deafening roar, its gaze fixed on V-Kar's kill. It was not the first time he had faced a rival predator, but this one was larger, stronger, and hungry.

V-Kar growled low in his throat, his claws curling into the earth. His mind raced as he calculated his options. He could fight, but even his cunning had limits against such a beast. Or he could flee, abandoning his hard - won prize - a thought that ignited a fiery anger within him.

He chose neither.

Instead, V-Kar darted forward, dragging the carcass toward the edge of a rocky ravine. The theropod snarled and charged, its massive jaws snapping inches from V-Kar's tail. But as the beast lunged, V-Kar released the kill, sending it tumbling over the edge.

The theropod hesitated, its instincts warring with its hunger. Then, with a frustrated snarl, it turned and stomped away, leaving V-Kar to slink back into the shadows.

The Clan's Shadow

V-Kar returned to the safety of a secluded cave, its walls damp with condensation and streaked with mineral veins that glistened in the dim light. His kill had been lost, but survival mattered more than pride.

The cave was not his alone. Other reptilians lingered here, their eyes gleaming in the darkness. They hissed low greetings, acknowledging his return but little else. V-Kar was tolerated, but he was not liked.

"Another hunt, another loss," sneered a slender reptilian with mottled green scales. Her tone dripped with disdain. "Perhaps you should let the theropods do your hunting."

V-Kar said nothing. He moved past her, his claws scraping the stone floor, and settled near the far wall. He licked the remnants of blood from his snout, his thoughts simmering.

He had survived. That was what mattered. But survival was not enough - not for V-Kar. One day, he would be more than a mere hunter scraping by in the jungle. One day, he would rise above them all.

V-KAR'S EPIC

As the distant cries of the jungle faded into the night, V-Kar closed his eyes, his tail curling tightly around him. The scent of damp stone and the faint metallic tang of his earlier kill lingered in the air.

Tomorrow, he would hunt again. And tomorrow, he would grow stronger.

Chapter 2: The Shadows Of Ambition

The jungle sang with life as dawn broke, spilling golden light over the canopy. Moist air clung to the world, carrying the rich, earthy scent of damp soil and the sweet tang of flowering cycads. V-Kar stood at the edge of a rocky outcrop, his claws curling over its edge, his eyes scanning the horizon. His emerald-scaled hide gleamed in the light, and his golden eyes narrowed with predatory focus.

This was his world, raw and untamed. He was not content merely to survive within it. V-Kar was a hunter, but his ambitions stretched beyond the kill. Where others saw prey, he saw opportunity. Where others accepted their place, he sought to reshape it.

Below him, the jungle stretched endlessly, a sea of greens and golds alive with movement. Somewhere within it, another challenge awaited - another step on the path that only he could see.

V-KAR'S EPIC

The Silent Rivalry

The morning hunt was already underway. The others in his clan - sleek and silent reptilians with darkened hides that blended into the underbrush - moved as one. V-Kar watched them from above, his tail flicking with quiet irritation.

They were predictable, hunting in coordinated packs to bring down prey too large for any single hunter. It was efficient, but to V-Kar, it reeked of submission. To rely on others, to move as a single organism, was to forfeit individuality, strength, and power.

Among them was Thaila, her mottled scales casting shadows across the forest floor as she led the pack. Her movements were fluid, her commands sharp, and the others obeyed without question. Thaila was not merely their leader - she was their symbol, their anchor.

V-Kar hated her for it.

She had everything he lacked: loyalty, respect, trust. Yet to him, those things were chains, binding her to the will of others. He sought something greater - absolute freedom, the ability to shape his own destiny without restraint.

The Lone Hunt

As the pack moved deeper into the jungle, V-Kar turned away. He had no interest in their coordinated hunts. He preferred to hunt alone, his own instincts untethered by the need to cooperate or share.

The jungle swallowed him as he moved silently through the underbrush. His senses sharpened: the faint rustle of leaves betrayed a small creature scurrying nearby; the earthy tang of overturned soil hinted at a large herbivore's recent passage.

V-Kar followed the scent, his claws flexing as he crept closer. The jungle opened into a small clearing, where a lone parasaurolophus stood grazing, its great horned crest casting a shadow over the lush ferns.

V-Kar's breath slowed. He crouched low, his muscles coiling like springs. Every sound faded, his focus narrowing to the steady rise and fall of the creature's flank.

Then, in a blur of motion, he struck.

The Spoils Of Victory

The parasaurolophus let out a shrill cry as V-Kar's claws tore into its hide. It staggered, but his jaws found its throat before it could escape. Warm blood sprayed across his snout as the creature collapsed, its body trembling before falling still.

V-Kar stood over his kill, his chest heaving, his senses still alive with the thrill of the hunt. The jungle around him felt distant, the cries of startled birds and the rustle of unseen predators mere background noise to his triumph.

But his satisfaction was short-lived.

The familiar scent of another reptilian reached him, sharp and intrusive. He turned, his eyes narrowing as Thaila emerged from the shadows. Her gaze swept over the scene, lingering on the fallen prey before meeting his.

"Impressive," she said, her tone even. "But reckless."

V-Kar's claws tightened against the ground. "Reckless only to those who lack the strength to succeed."

Thaila stepped closer, her movements deliberate. "And what do you gain from this strength? The pack grows stronger when we hunt together. Your victories only feed yourself."

"Exactly," V-Kar snapped. "I hunt for myself, not for others. Strength is not meant to be shared - it is meant to be claimed."

Thaila's eyes narrowed. "You speak of strength as if it sets you apart. But strength without purpose is nothing. The pack survives because we stand together. Alone, even the strongest fall."

V-Kar's tail lashed behind him. He turned away, his claws sinking into the blood-soaked earth. "Then fall with your pack, Thaila. I'll rise alone."

Seeds Of Ambition

As V-Kar dragged his kill into the underbrush, Thaila watched him go, her expression unreadable. His words lingered, a challenge that echoed in the depths of her mind.

V-Kar's ambition was dangerous - his refusal to see beyond himself, his belief that strength could stand unassisted. But she could not deny the power in his gaze, the raw determination that burned within him.

V-Kar, for his part, did not look back. He did not care for Thaila's approval or her warnings. She was bound by the pack, trapped by her belief in unity. He had no such chains.

As he moved deeper into the jungle, his thoughts burned with a single desire: to rise. He would carve his path with tooth and claw, and when the time came, even the strongest would kneel before him.

V-KAR'S EPIC

Chapter 3: The Breath Of The Jungle

The prehistoric world was alive with vibrant chaos. The jungle was not merely a collection of trees and ferns; it was a living, breathing entity, its rhythms and pulses as intricate as any creature within it. The air was thick and heavy, filled with scents that hinted at life unseen: the musk of predators, the sweetness of blooming cycads, the metallic tang of water pooling in hidden grottoes.

V-Kar prowled through the undergrowth, his scales glistening with dew, each step deliberate and soundless. The jungle's sounds surrounded him - the calls of pterosaurs wheeling high above, the rustle of small creatures scurrying beneath the foliage, the occasional distant roar that reverberated like thunder.

His yellow eyes scanned the landscape, attuned to every movement. To survive in this world was to understand its language, and V-Kar spoke it fluently. Every rustle of leaves, every shift in the wind carried meaning, a warning or an opportunity.

The River's Edge

The jungle opened suddenly, revealing the glimmer of a wide river cutting through the landscape. Its waters flowed swiftly, carrying the earthy scent of mud and algae. Along its banks, clusters of prehistoric dragonflies hovered, their iridescent wings catching the sunlight in flashes of green and blue.

A family of ankylosaurs waded near the shallows, their armored backs gleaming like polished stone. The largest among them - likely a matriarch - stood watch, her club-like tail twitching in warning. V-Kar lingered at the edge of the tree line, his presence masked by shadows.

He had no intention of attacking; the ankylosaurs were too well-armored, their defenses too formidable. But he watched with sharp interest, noting how even the most invulnerable creatures relied on their environment for safety. The jungle was a delicate balance, and V-Kar was determined to tip it in his favor.

A Clash Of Titans

The calm was broken by the arrival of a predator - a massive, scarred allosaurus bursting from the underbrush. Its roar split the air, sending birds shrieking from the canopy. The ankylosaurs bristled, their tails swinging as they formed a protective circle.

The allosaurus lunged, its teeth flashing, but the matriarch struck with her tail, the impact resounding like a crack of thunder. The predator staggered but did not retreat.

V-Kar watched intently, his claws curling into the dirt. This was the jungle's truth: strength was fleeting, survival a constant contest. Even the mightiest fell if they miscalculated.

The fight raged on, the air thick with the scent of blood and the primal roars of combat. When it ended, the allosaurus limped away, defeated but alive, while the ankylosaurs resumed their wary watch.

V-KAR'S EPIC

The Mountain's Call

Days later, V-Kar found himself at the base of a towering mountain, its jagged peaks shrouded in mist. The air here was cooler, carrying the crisp bite of mineral-rich stone. Streams trickled down its slopes, their waters glinting like silver as they fed into the jungle below.

This was a place of power, a vantage point that promised dominance over the surrounding terrain. V-Kar climbed, his claws gripping the rocky surface, his muscles burning with effort.

When he reached the summit, the view took his breath away. The jungle stretched endlessly in all directions, a living sea of green. Rivers wound like veins through the land, and distant herds moved like specks on the horizon. The wind roared around him, carrying with it the scent of possibility.

This was the world he sought to command.

The Sky Hunters

From his perch, V-Kar observed the skies, where pterosaurs soared with graceful power. Their calls echoed across the peaks, their leathery wings casting shadows over the cliffs.

One in particular caught his eye - a massive quetzalcoatlus, its wingspan rivaling that of a small sail. It dove sharply, snatching an unwary protoceratops from the ground with talons like curved daggers.

The jungle's sky was as dangerous as its ground, yet V-Kar felt no fear. These predators were rivals, yes, but they were also lessons. Their mastery of the air was a reminder that dominance required adaptability.

The Fire In The Night

One night, the jungle erupted in flame. Lightning had struck a dry patch of forest, igniting an inferno that roared through the undergrowth with terrifying speed. The air was thick with smoke, choking and acrid, and the crackling of burning wood drowned out the cries of fleeing creatures.

V-Kar ran, his senses sharpened by urgency. The heat singed his scales, and the acrid scent of charred vegetation burned his nostrils. Yet even in the chaos, he observed. The fire was not merely destruction; it was transformation. The jungle would regrow, its balance restored by the very force that had consumed it.

This was the nature of the world: endless cycles of destruction and renewal. V-Kar's mind burned with the realization. To command this world, he would need to master these cycles, bending them to his will.

The Whisper Of Time

Years passed in the jungle, each day honing V-Kar's instincts and sharpening his resolve. He grew stronger, more cunning, his name whispered among his kin as both a warning and a challenge. Yet, for all his dominance, there was one mystery he could not unravel: the strange markings he occasionally found carved into stone thorough the cave.

V-KAR'S EPIC

They were not natural, nor were they the work of the pack. The markings glowed faintly in the moonlight, their patterns intricate and deliberate.

One night, as he studied these carvings, a figure emerged from the shadows. It was a reptilian like him, but older, their eyes gleaming with knowledge.

"You've wondered what they mean," the figure said, their voice low and measured.

V-Kar tensed but did not strike. "Speak."

The figure smiled faintly. "They are messages, left by your descendants. Messages from a future you cannot yet comprehend."

V-Kar's claws curled into the stone. "Why would my descendants leave messages for me?"

"Because you are their beginning," the figure said. "And they are your end."

<u>Chapter 4: The Unseen Threats</u>

The jungle's morning light filtered through the dense canopy, casting speckled patterns across the ground. The air was alive with sound - the squawking of pterosaurs, the buzzing hum of insects, and the occasional distant roar of predators marking their territory. V-Kar moved silently through the undergrowth, his golden eyes sharp, every nerve attuned to his surroundings.

This was his world, but he had long learned that to thrive here, one had to be more than just a hunter. The jungle's threats were not always visible. Some were heard before they were seen; others gave no warning at all. And it was these unseen dangers that tested him most.

<u>The Death In The Water</u>

The river wound lazily through the jungle, its surface gleaming like molten silver in the sunlight. V-Kar crouched at its edge, the soft squelch of mud beneath his claws blending with the burbling of the water. His reflection stared back at him - a predator's face, sleek and sharp, framed by scales that shimmered like polished stone.

But V-Kar did not drink. He knew better. The water might appear calm, but it concealed a silent killer.

Just beneath the surface, shadows moved. A pair of eyes broke the waterline, dark and unblinking. The sarcosuchus, an ancient crocodilian larger than a small sailboat, lay in wait. Its body was perfectly still, its long, jagged snout barely visible.

V-Kar hissed softly, stepping back. He would not be its prey.

Instead, he picked up a rock and hurled it into the water. The splash was immediate, the sarcosuchus lunging toward the disturbance with terrifying speed. The water churned violently, the beast's jaws snapping shut on empty air before it disappeared beneath the surface once more.

V-Kar smirked. Let others fall to its hunger. He would drink elsewhere.

The Swarm

As the day wore on, the jungle grew hotter, the humidity clinging like a second skin. V-Kar moved through a dense patch of cycads, the scent of their sap thick in the air. His claws scraped against the bark as he passed, leaving faint marks - a habit of his, a way of leaving traces of his presence in the jungle.

But something was wrong. The usual hum of insects was missing, replaced by an eerie silence.

V-Kar froze, his body going still as he scanned the trees. Then he heard it: a faint droning sound, rising like a distant storm.

A moment later, the swarm appeared.

It came like a living cloud, a mass of insects so thick it blocked out the sunlight. The air was filled with the metallic buzz of their wings, the acrid stench of their bodies. These were no ordinary bugs; they were meganeura, dragonflies the size of eagles, their jaws sharp enough to tear flesh.

V-Kar ran.

The jungle blurred around him as he sprinted, his claws tearing at the ground, his breaths coming fast and shallow. The swarm followed, their buzzing growing louder, closer. He dodged between trees, leaped over roots, and finally dove into a hollow log.

The swarm passed overhead, their wings rattling like dry leaves. V-Kar waited, his chest heaving, the earthy scent of the log filling his nostrils. When the sound faded, he crawled out, his scales streaked with dirt.

He hissed softly, vowing to avoid this part of the jungle for a while.

The Soundless Danger

The jungle was alive with countless sounds, but V-Kar had learned to fear the absence of them. Silence often meant a predator - one that moved with such precision that it left no trace of its approach.

It was late afternoon when he felt it: the quiet.

V-Kar crouched low, his muscles tense. The usual hum of insects had faded, and even the distant cries of pterosaurs were absent. The air itself felt heavy, the jungle holding its breath.

Then he saw it.

V-KAR'S EPIC

A raptor pack moved through the underbrush, their mottled hides blending seamlessly with the foliage. Their movements were graceful, almost serpentine, their claws clicking softly against the ground.

V-Kar remained perfectly still, his yellow eyes following their every move. Raptors were fast, intelligent, and deadly in groups. A single mistake would be fatal.

The pack leader paused, its head tilting as it sniffed the air. Its eyes locked on V-Kar's position, and for a moment, time seemed to freeze.

Then the raptor let out a piercing screech, and the pack charged.

V-Kar sprang into action, darting through the jungle with the raptors in pursuit. He weaved between trees, his claws finding purchase on the rough bark as he climbed higher. The raptors followed, their snarls echoing through the canopy.

But V-Kar was faster. He leaped to another tree, then another, until the pack fell behind, their screeches fading into the distance.

When he finally stopped, perched on a thick branch high above the jungle floor, he let out a low growl of frustration.

The jungle never let him rest.

<u>The Lesson Of The Day</u>

As the sun dipped toward the horizon, casting the jungle in shades of gold and orange, V-Kar made his way to a secluded clearing. Here, the air was still, the ground soft with moss. The scent of nearby blooms was sweet but faint, blending with the earthy aroma of damp wood.

He crouched near a small pool, its surface clear and still. He drank deeply, the cool water soothing his parched throat.

Today had tested him, as every day did. The sarcosuchus, the swarm, the raptors - all reminders that even the strongest could fall if they were not vigilant.

But V-Kar did not resent the jungle for its dangers. He thrived on them. Every threat, every challenge sharpened him, honed his instincts, and fueled his ambition.

As the stars began to appear, their faint light filtering through the canopy, V-Kar lay back on the moss, his tail curling around him. The jungle hummed softly, its rhythms a lullaby for those strong enough to survive its trials.

V-Kar closed his eyes, his thoughts simmering. Tomorrow would bring new dangers, new lessons. And he would face them all.

V-KAR'S EPIC

Chapter 5: The Ways Of The Tribe

The reptilian tribes of the prehistoric world lived by an unspoken code, one carved into their very survival. Loyalty, tenuous as it was, bound them to their groups. A lizardkin alone was as good as dead. The jungle, with its countless dangers, spared no solitary creature, no matter how strong or cunning.

The tribe offered a fragile safety. In numbers, they hunted, defended their dens, and raised their young. Yet their loyalty was not born of affection or kinship - it was a reluctant allegiance, driven by the knowledge that unity was the only shield against the jungle's unrelenting hunger.

Among themselves, the reptilians were territorial and wary. Dominance and submission dictated their relationships, with disputes often settled through combat or silent acknowledgment of strength. But even the strongest had limits, and those who broke the tribe's delicate balance risked banishment - a fate worse than death.

The Cave's Hierarchy

V-Kar's cave was no different. It housed a small tribe of lizardkin, no more than fifteen in total. The cave's interior was dim and damp, its walls streaked with mineral veins and claw marks left by generations past. A faint, acrid smell of reptilian musk filled the air, mingling with the earthy scent of damp stone.

At the center of the cave lay Thaila, the tribe's de facto leader. Her presence commanded respect, her movements sharp and deliberate. The others followed her lead not out of devotion, but because her strength ensured their survival.

V-Kar had never truly belonged. He was tolerated because he was a skilled hunter, his kills feeding the tribe. But his ambition set him apart, his refusal to submit marking him as a threat to the fragile unity.

For weeks, tension had simmered between him and Thaila. It had begun with words, barbed and challenging, each testing the other's dominance. But V-Kar wanted more. He sought to claim Thaila as his mate - not out of affection, but as a symbol of his power.

Thaila, however, was no prize to be won.

The Confrontation

It happened at dusk, as the jungle's shadows lengthened and the cave filled with the low murmurs of the tribe settling in for the night.

V-Kar approached Thaila, his claws clicking softly against the stone. The others watched from the edges of the cave, their eyes gleaming with curiosity and unease.

"You should choose me," V-Kar said, his voice low and firm. "I am the strongest. Together, we would lead the tribe to dominance."

Thaila's eyes narrowed, her tail twitching. "You mistake strength for worth. I choose no one, and certainly not you."

The rejection stung, but V-Kar's anger burned hotter than his pride. He stepped closer, his claws flexing. "You have no choice."

Thaila's hiss was sharp and venomous. "You would dare?"

The moment hung heavy, the air in the cave thick with tension. Then V-Kar lunged, his claws reaching for Thaila, his intent clear.

But she was faster.

Strength Meets Strength

Thaila's tail struck first, sweeping V-Kar's legs out from under him. He hit the ground hard, the impact jarring his senses, but he recovered quickly, rolling to his feet.

The two circled each other, their movements deliberate and predatory. The others watched in silence, their expressions unreadable.

V-Kar struck again, his claws raking through the air, but Thaila dodged with fluid precision. She countered with a swipe of her own, her claws grazing his shoulder.

"You are a fool," Thaila spat, her voice a venomous growl. "You think power is taken, but true strength is earned."

V-Kar growled, his frustration mounting. He lunged again, but Thaila met him head-on, their claws locking in a brutal clash. For a moment, it seemed as though neither would yield.

But then Thaila's strength surged, her tail whipping around to strike V-Kar's side. He staggered, and she pressed her advantage, slamming him to the ground with a powerful shove.

The Sentence

Thaila stood over V-Kar, her claws pressed to his throat. "You have broken the tribe's code," she said, her voice cold and resolute. "You threaten our unity, our survival. For this, you are no longer one of us."

The words struck harder than any blow. V-Kar stared up at her, his chest heaving, his pride shattered.

"You banish me?" he hissed.

"Yes," Thaila said, stepping back. "Leave, or face the consequences."

The others did not speak, but their silence was an agreement. V-Kar had crossed a line, and now he would pay the price.

He rose slowly, his claws digging into the stone. His eyes burned with anger, but he said nothing. Turning, he stalked out of the cave, the cold night air hitting him like a wall.

Alone In The Jungle

For the first time, V-Kar was truly alone. The jungle stretched before him, vast and indifferent. The sounds of the night were louder now: the distant roars of predators, the rustle of unseen dangers.

The scent of damp earth filled his nostrils, mingling with the metallic tang of his own blood. The stars above offered no comfort, their cold light a reminder of the isolation that now defined him.

But as V-Kar moved deeper into the jungle, his anger began to harden into something else. He had been cast out, humiliated, but he was not defeated.

"They will regret this," he growled to himself, his claws flexing. "I will rise, and they will kneel."

The jungle's shadows closed around him, and V-Kar disappeared into the night.

Chapter 6: The Night's Shadows

The jungle was alive with sound as night fell. Leaves rustled with the passage of small creatures, their movements hidden in the dense underbrush. The distant roar of a predator sent birds screeching into the sky, their silhouettes stark against the pale glow of the moon. Yet V-Kar heard little of it. His own heavy breaths and the pounding of his heart drowned out the world around him.

He ran, his muscles burning, his claws sinking into the soft earth with each desperate stride. The damp, muggy air clung to his scales, mingling with the metallic tang of his blood from where Thaila had struck him. He didn't know where he was going, nor did he care. He only knew that he needed to keep moving.

The shame of his banishment weighed on him like a stone. His chest ached with the memory of Thaila's cold dismissal, and the quiet agreement of the others echoed in his mind. The tribe had rejected him - rejected his strength, his ambition.

When exhaustion finally overtook him, V-Kar collapsed against the trunk of a towering cycad. The rough bark scratched at his back as he slid to the ground, his tail curling weakly around him. The scents of the jungle filled his nostrils - wet earth, decaying leaves, the faint musk of nearby predators - but none of it registered.

His eyes fluttered shut, and for the first time in his life, V-Kar dreamed.

V-KAR'S EPIC

The Symbols Of The Past

The dream began in silence, the jungle's sounds replaced by a deep, otherworldly hum. Shapes and symbols floated before him, their edges glowing faintly with light. They were the same markings he had seen etched into the cave walls - a mystery he had dismissed as irrelevant.

Now, they pulsed with meaning, though their purpose eluded him.

In the dream, a figure stepped forward, cloaked in shadows yet unmistakably reptilian. Its eyes gleamed with an ancient knowledge, piercing through V-Kar's pride and fear.

"You've wondered what they mean," the figure said, its voice calm yet unyielding.

V-Kar recognized the words. This was the conversation from the symbols he had seen, the one he hadn't been part of - until now.

"They are messages," the figure continued, "left by your descendants. Messages from a future you cannot yet comprehend."

V-Kar growled softly, his claws curling as if ready to strike. "Why would my descendants leave messages for me?"

The figure's voice deepened, its tone both patient and commanding. "Because you are their beginning. And they are your end."

The Shame Of Failure

The dream shifted, the symbols fading into darkness. V-Kar found himself back in the cave, standing before Thaila. Her eyes were cold, her stance unwavering.

"You have no choice," his dream-self hissed, his voice laced with anger and desperation.

Thaila's response struck harder than any blow: "You mistake strength for worth."

Her words echoed as the scene replayed, over and over. Each time, V-Kar lunged, and each time, he was cast down.

The shame clawed at him, coiling around his thoughts like a serpent. His ambition, his arrogance, had led to his downfall. He had been cast out, not for his weakness but for his inability to see beyond himself.

The Symbols Return

The symbols returned, glowing brighter this time, their edges sharper. They seemed to pulse in time with his heartbeat, each shape drawing him closer.

"What do they mean?" V-Kar asked, his voice breaking the silence.

The figure appeared again, its presence overwhelming. "You will not understand until you seek. The jungle has its truths, but the stones hold deeper ones."

V-Kar's claws flexed, his tail lashing. "I will find them."

The figure's eyes gleamed. "You will. But the path is not easy, and the answers will demand more of you than you yet possess."

The hum grew louder, the symbols spinning faster, their light engulfing V-Kar. He opened his mouth to speak, but the dream dissolved, leaving him in the void.

Waking To The Jungle

V-Kar awoke with a start, his chest heaving. The jungle was quiet now, the nocturnal symphony reduced to the occasional chirp of insects and the distant call of a pterosaur.

He sat up, his claws gripping the damp ground as he tried to steady himself. The dream lingered in his mind, vivid and insistent. Reptilians did not dream. Their minds were grounded in the physical world, their senses rooted in smell and sound, not the intangible.

Yet, V-Kar had dreamed. And the symbols - those glowing shapes - demanded his attention.

He rose slowly, his body aching from his flight through the jungle. The scent of moss and damp stone filled his nostrils, mingling with the faint musk of nearby predators. Yet his focus was elsewhere.

For weeks, the dream haunted him. The symbols and the figure's words replayed in his mind as he moved through the jungle. He hunted, he fought, he survived, but his thoughts always returned to the markings.

"What do they mean?" he growled to himself, his claws scraping against the bark of a nearby tree.

The Abandoned Cave

It was near the edge of a rocky outcrop that he finally found it: a cave, its entrance jagged and overgrown with vines. The air here was cooler, carrying the metallic tang of stone and the faint sweetness of nearby blooms.

Cautiously, V-Kar stepped inside. The cave was dark, its walls slick with condensation. Stalactites hung like teeth from the ceiling, and the floor was littered with scattered stones.

But it was empty. No scents of other reptilians, no signs of predators. This place had been abandoned long ago.

V-Kar moved deeper, his eyes adjusting to the dim light. And then he saw them - the markings.

The walls were etched with the same glowing symbols from his dream, their light faint but unmistakable. They pulsed softly, as if waiting for him.

V-Kar's breath caught, his claws flexing as he approached. For the first time in weeks, he felt something other than anger or shame.

He felt purpose.

Chapter 7: Secrets In The Stone

The cave was quiet, the only sound the occasional drip of water from the jagged stalactites above. V-Kar's claws clicked softly against the damp stone floor as he moved deeper, his yellow eyes fixed on the glowing symbols etched into the walls.

The markings pulsed faintly, their arrangement unlike anything he had ever seen. They were clustered together, arranged in patterns that seemed deliberate, though their meaning eluded him.

"This must have been the tribe's cave once," V-Kar muttered to himself, his voice echoing softly in the empty space. He crouched beside a cluster of symbols, his claws tracing their grooves.

The thought of his tribe living here felt strangely fitting. The cave was smaller than their current one, its walls narrower, its air heavier with the scent of wet stone and moss. They must have outgrown it, moving on when their numbers swelled.

But the symbols - they were different. V-Kar had seen claw marks and crude etchings before, left by generations of reptilians, but these were intricate, deliberate. They were not scratches made in passing; they were crafted with purpose.

The Symbols' Mystery
V-Kar studied the symbols, his mind racing. The markings seemed to repeat in patterns, some jagged and sharp, others

curved and flowing. He had no idea what they meant, but their arrangement stirred something in him.

"They must have used these," he said, his voice low, "to plan hunts. To teach… something forbidden."

He could almost see it: his ancestors, gathered in this cave, their claws tracing the symbols as they whispered secrets to one another. Perhaps they had used these symbols to craft plans too dangerous to speak aloud, to teach magics too powerful to be shared openly.

The thought sent a thrill through V-Kar. If the symbols held the key to something greater - something beyond brute strength - he could use it.

"This," he growled, "is how I will rise."

Masking His Scent

The air grew cooler as V-Kar moved deeper into the cave, the light from the entrance fading into darkness. The scent of damp stone grew stronger, mingling with the earthy tang of mud.

At the far end of the cave, he found a shallow pool, its surface rippling faintly as water dripped from above. The mud here was thick and cold, clinging to his claws as he knelt beside it.

V-Kar reached down, scooping the mud into his hands. He smeared it over his scales, masking his scent. It was a habit born of survival - predators could follow the faintest trace, and V-Kar had no intention of being found.

V-KAR'S EPIC

As the mud cooled his skin, his mind returned to the symbols. They called to him, their faint glow seeming to pulse in time with his thoughts.

"This was their secret," he murmured, his voice barely above a whisper. "A way to lead, not through strength alone, but through knowledge. Through power no one else could understand."

A Story Forms

As V-Kar sat in the cool darkness, the symbols began to take shape in his mind. They were no longer random marks on the wall; they were pieces of a story - a story he would write himself.

He imagined his ancestors, their scales glinting in the faint light of the cave, gathered around these symbols. They must have used them to share forbidden knowledge, to plan hunts that no other tribe could match.

Perhaps they had discovered magics - ways to twist the jungle's dangers to their will, to control the beasts that roamed its shadows. These secrets had been left behind, hidden in the symbols, waiting for someone strong enough to uncover them.

"That someone is me," V-Kar growled.

He rose to his feet, his claws flexing. He would not return to the tribe begging for forgiveness. He would create his own tribe - a tribe built on secrecy and fear, on knowledge and power. He would use the symbols to rule, not just by strength, but by a force greater than any reptilian had ever known.

Recruiting The Outcasts

But V-Kar could not do it alone. He needed others - those desperate enough to follow him, those willing to betray the tribe for the promise of something greater.

He returned to the jungle under the cover of night, his scent masked by the mud drying on his scales. The jungle's nocturnal symphony surrounded him - the rustle of leaves, the distant roars of predators - but V-Kar moved with purpose.

His first target was Torrak, a wiry male whose cunning was matched only by his lack of respect among the tribe. Torrak was tolerated but despised, his sharp tongue and cowardly nature making him an outcast even among his kin.

V-Kar approached him silently, his claws scraping the bark of a tree to announce his presence. Torrak spun around, his eyes wide with fear, but V-Kar's voice was calm.

"You don't belong there," V-Kar said, his tone low and commanding. "But with me, you can have what they'll never give you: power."

Torrak hesitated, his tail twitching. "What do you want from me?"

"Loyalty," V-Kar replied. "And silence."

V-KAR'S EPIC

Brutality's Edge

Over the next week, V-Kar recruited five more outcasts. Each was chosen for their desperation, their resentment of the tribe that had cast them aside. But V-Kar's methods were not gentle.

When Zenn, a broad-shouldered female, resisted his offer, V-Kar struck without hesitation. His claws raked across her snout, leaving deep gashes that oozed dark blood.

"You think they'll protect you?" he growled, his voice dripping with contempt. "You're nothing to them. But to me, you're a weapon - a blade they've thrown away, ready to cut deeper than they ever could."

Zenn snarled, her chest heaving with rage, but her defiance wavered as the truth of his words settled over her. The tribe had cast her aside, ignoring her strength in favor of those more agreeable, more loyal to Thaila's rigid order.

"Fine," she spat, her claws flexing. "But if you betray me, V-Kar, I'll tear you apart."

V-Kar's grin was sharp, his teeth glinting in the faint moonlight. "Good. I wouldn't expect anything less."

The Foundation Of A New Tribe

By the end of the week, six outcasts stood at V-Kar's side. They were scarred, bitter, and mistrustful - perfect for his purposes. He led them back to the abandoned cave, their movements silent and deliberate as they slipped away from the tribe's watchful eyes.

Inside the cave, the symbols glowed faintly, their light casting strange shadows across the walls. V-Kar stood before his followers, his claws tracing the markings as he spoke.

"This is our future," he said, his voice low and commanding. "These symbols hold the secrets of our ancestors - secrets the tribe has forgotten, secrets we will reclaim."

The outcasts exchanged wary glances, their eyes flicking between V-Kar and the glowing symbols.

"What do they mean?" Torrak asked, his voice tinged with suspicion.

"They mean power," V-Kar replied, his gaze unyielding. "Our ancestors used these symbols to plan hunts, to wield magics the tribe fears to this day. Together, we will uncover their secrets. And when we do, we will be unstoppable."

The cave fell silent, the faint dripping of water the only sound. Then Zenn stepped forward, her claws scraping the stone floor.

"And what happens when the tribe comes for us?" she asked, her voice steady but sharp.

V-Kar's smile was cold. "Let them come. We will show them what it means to fear."

V-KAR'S EPIC

A New Path

As the night deepened, V-Kar's new tribe settled into the cave, their shapes blending into the shadows. The air was thick with tension, the unspoken weight of their decision hanging over them. They had chosen to follow V-Kar, to abandon the safety of the larger tribe for the promise of something greater.

For V-Kar, the path was clear. The symbols would be his guide, their secrets the foundation of his rule. Through magic, secrecy, and brutality, he would build a new order - one where strength was more than muscle, and loyalty was demanded, not earned.

As he lay back against the cold stone, the faint glow of the symbols reflected in his golden eyes, V-Kar felt the stirrings of a new ambition.

He had been cast out, humiliated, but that was the past. Now, he would rise.

And when the time came, he would not just lead a tribe. He would rule a kingdom.

Chapter 8: The Keeper Of Forgotten Tales

The air in the abandoned cave hung heavy with dampness, the faint glow of the symbols casting jagged shadows on the walls. V-Kar sat at the center, his tail curled around him, his claws tapping the stone floor in thought. The six outcasts lingered nearby, their movements quiet, their eyes wary.

It was the oldest among them - a grizzled reptilian with dull, scarred scales - who broke the silence. His voice rasped like wind over dry leaves, his tone low and deliberate.

"You think you've found something new," the elder said, his gaze fixed on V-Kar. "But these symbols? They've been here longer than any of us. Longer than the tribe itself."

V-Kar's eyes narrowed. "What do you know of them, old one?"

The elder chuckled softly, a sound like dry bark cracking. "I know more than you think. I remember the time when these symbols weren't just marks on a wall. They were power - real power. But that was before your time, before even mine. The stories…" He trailed off, his eyes gleaming with something between mischief and nostalgia.

"Tell me," V-Kar demanded, his voice sharp.

The elder leaned back against the wall, his tail curling lazily. "Very well. But don't blame me if the truth unsettles you."

V-KAR'S EPIC

The Tale Of The Magic Emperor

The elder's voice dropped to a whisper, drawing the others closer despite themselves.

"Long ago," he began, "before the jungle swallowed everything, there was a ruler - a magic emperor who commanded fear itself. He was no ordinary reptilian. He could look at an enemy and make them vanish without a trace. His gaze was said to pierce the soul, leaving nothing behind but shadows."

The younger outcasts exchanged uneasy glances, but V-Kar's expression remained cold and calculating.

"And these symbols?" V-Kar asked, his claws tracing one of the glowing marks. "What part did they play?"

The elder gestured to the walls, his claw sweeping over the patterns.   "These were his spells," he said, his voice reverent. "The secrets of his power. But that knowledge has been lost. The tribe feared it, destroyed it. Only scraps remain - fragments of a greatness we'll never see again."

V-Kar hissed softly, his tail flicking. The story reeked of exaggeration, its details too grand to be entirely true. Yet, there was something about the elder's tone - something that hinted at a kernel of truth buried beneath the tale.

"You speak of power," V-Kar said, his voice sharp. "But words and marks don't make prey fall or enemies flee. What did the emperor use? What was his weapon?"

The elder smiled faintly, his eyes glinting in the dim light. "Ah, you're smarter than you look, V-Kar. You see through the stories. Good. Let me show you something real."

The Spark And The Flame

The elder rose slowly, his movements deliberate. He reached into a small pouch tied to his waist, pulling out a jagged stone flecked with dark, oily streaks. He held it up, his claws glinting in the light of the symbols.

"This," he said, "is what the emperor's enemies feared most. Not spells, not magic - fire."

"Fire?" V-Kar scoffed, though he leaned forward, intrigued.

The elder crouched by a shallow pool where dark liquid oozed from the cave walls - crude oil, its pungent scent filling the air. He dipped his claws into it, smearing the thick substance over a dry patch of moss on the floor.

"Watch," the elder said.

He struck the jagged stone against his claw, the sound sharp and grating. A spark leaped from the stone, landing on the oil-soaked moss. Instantly, flames erupted, their light casting flickering shadows across the cave.

The younger outcasts recoiled, their eyes wide with shock. V-Kar, however, stepped closer, his gaze fixed on the fire.

"It's not magic," the elder said, his voice calm. "But to those who don't understand, it might as well be. The emperor's power wasn't in spells. It was in knowing what others feared and making them believe he controlled the impossible."

V-Kar's eyes gleamed as he watched the flames dance.

The Seed Of Ambition

As the fire burned low, V-Kar crouched beside the elder, his claws tapping the stone. "You're saying he used tricks. Lies."

"Lies are powerful," the elder replied. "But only if you make them real enough to believe. Fire like this? To the tribe, it would seem like magic. To your enemies, it would be terror."

V-Kar nodded slowly, his mind racing. "Show me everything," he demanded.

Over the next few days, the elder taught V-Kar how to find crude oil, how to strike a spark with a flint stone, and how to control the flames. He showed him how to coat the inside of his mouth with oil, spitting it into the fire to create a plume of flame.

By the end of the week, V-Kar carried a small pouch of oil and a flint stone at all times. To his followers, he seemed untouchable, his every step brimming with the promise of power.

V-KAR'S EPIC

The End Of The Elder

But the elder's usefulness had run its course. The others resented him, his smugness and knowledge setting him apart even among outcasts.

One night, V-Kar confronted him. "You've served your purpose," he said, his voice cold. "You're not one of us. You never were."

The elder chuckled softly, though his eyes betrayed fear. "You'd kill the one who gave you power?"

"No," V-Kar said, baring his teeth. "I'll kill the one who thinks it's still his."

The fight was short, brutal. V-Kar's claws found the elder's throat, silencing him forever.

As his body slumped to the ground, V-Kar turned to the others. "The fire is ours now," he said. "And with it, we will take everything."

The Flame Of Fear

In the days that followed, V-Kar grew bold. With the flint stone in one claw and oil hidden in his pouch, he seemed to command fire itself. He spat flames at the jungle's shadows, his outcasts watching in awe.

Word began to spread among the tribes of a reptilian who breathed fire, who commanded the ancient magics of their ancestors. V-Kar encouraged the rumors, letting fear and uncertainty do what strength alone could not.

V-KAR'S EPIC

The jungle was no longer just a home. It was his stage, and the fire his weapon.

V-Kar was no longer a mere outcast. He was becoming something far more dangerous.

Chapter 9: The Hidden Inferno

The jungle continued its ceaseless hum of life, but now, deep in its shadows, something new stirred. V-Kar's band grew, hidden beneath the dense canopy, their movements veiled by secrecy and fear. The abandoned cave became their haven, its glowing symbols etched into the minds of every new recruit.

V-Kar's strategy was simple: stay invisible, grow strong, and let the rumors spread like wildfire. While others speculated about a mysterious force lurking in the jungle, V-Kar's band operated in silence, eliminating threats before they could speak.

The Denial Of Fire

When whispers of a reptilian who breathed fire reached the larger tribe, Thaila dismissed them as myths. "Fire doesn't come from the breath," she told her hunters. "It comes from the storms."

Still, fear crept through the tribe. A patrol sent to investigate the rumors returned empty-clawed, speaking only of eerie quiet where the jungle should have been alive.

When asked directly about the fire, V-Kar's band denied everything. Torrak, now one of the most cunning of the six, spread deliberate confusion among any who questioned him.

"Fire?" he sneered to a wandering scout one evening. "If someone were breathing fire, don't you think you'd smell the burnt flesh?"

V-KAR'S EPIC

The scout left suspicious but unconvinced. V-Kar's band ensured no tracks or scents could lead back to their cave.

Recruiting In Shadows

Recruitment was a careful game. The six core members scouted for the discontented and desperate, seeking those who felt unseen or underestimated. Torrak, Zenn, and the others approached each potential recruit with a mix of promises and intimidation, gauging their willingness to join.

But not all were willing.

When a young reptilian named Skarn refused to join, he was dragged back to the cave. The six gathered in the dim light of the symbols, their eyes gleaming with predatory hunger. Skarn's pleas echoed off the walls, but V-Kar's voice cut through them, cold and sharp.

"You had a choice," V-Kar said, his claws clicking against the stone. "And you chose poorly."

What happened next was swift and brutal. The six tore into Skarn, their jaws and claws reducing him to nothing but bones. His screams were swallowed by the cave, never to reach the ears of the outside world.

Word spread quietly among the recruits: refusal was not an option.

V-KAR'S EPIC

A Growing Army

Over time, V-Kar's band grew. What had begun with six outcasts became a group of nearly two dozen, all bound by fear and the promise of power. Each member was tested, their loyalty forged through trials designed to strip away weakness.

The cave became a place of whispered rituals, where V-Kar stood before the glowing symbols and spoke of a new order. He painted visions of dominance and unity, of a tribe ruled by strength and secrecy. The fire became their unspoken weapon, its presence felt but never revealed beyond their ranks.

Those who faltered were consumed.

The Brutality Of Secrecy

The 5 other core members remained V-Kar's enforcers, their brutality ensuring that the growing band stayed loyal and quiet. When one recruit - a scrawny female named Krella - hesitated during a hunt, Zenn dragged her back to the cave.

V-Kar watched as the others surrounded Krella, their eyes cold. "Weakness has no place here," he said simply.

Krella begged for mercy, her cries filling the cave. But there was none to give. Zenn struck first, her claws tearing into Krella's side. Torrak followed, his jaws snapping. Within moments, Krella was gone, her blood staining the cave floor.

V-Kar looked over the remaining recruits, his gaze sharp. "This is what happens to those who fail," he said. "Remember it."

The Unseen Force

Despite their growing numbers, V-Kar's band remained invisible to the larger tribe. Their movements were calculated, their tracks erased. Those who ventured too close to their cave often disappeared, their fates never revealed.

V-Kar ensured that no pattern could be traced back to them. The fire, his most dangerous tool, was used sparingly and only in controlled circumstances. To the outside world, his band remained a myth - a shadow in the jungle.

But within the band, the fire was sacred. V-Kar carried his flint stone and oil at all times, his ability to ignite flames a symbol of his power. The others feared and revered him, believing the stories he spun about the symbols and the magic emperor.

V-Kar let them believe.

The Plan Takes Shape

As the band swelled in numbers, V-Kar began to see the shape of his plan. His tribe had cast him out, humiliated him, but they had also given him the opportunity to become something greater.

He would not merely take revenge. He would consume the tribe as his band consumed the weak. They would see his fire, his power, and they would kneel - or burn.

But for now, he would wait. Patience was another weapon, and V-Kar wielded it well.

As he stood before the symbols, their glow reflecting in his golden eyes, V-Kar allowed himself a rare smile.

"Soon," he whispered, the word carrying through the cave like a promise.

V-KAR'S EPIC

Chapter 10: The Choosing Of A Mate

The cave's atmosphere had changed. What had once been a desperate hideout for a handful of outcasts had transformed into a growing, volatile empire of fear and brutality. V-Kar, standing at the heart of it all, was no longer merely an outcast - he was a ruler. His presence commanded submission, his fire inspired terror, and his reputation was whispered with reverence and dread.

Among his growing followers, one stood out: Shyra, a lean, sharp-eyed female with a mind as quick as her movements. Shyra was different from the others - she spoke little, observed much, and had a cunning way of turning situations to her advantage.

V-Kar admired her intellect, though he kept his admiration hidden behind his cold, calculating demeanor. Yet his decision to make her his mate was not based solely on her wit. She was also the mate of Torrak, the only member of his original six followers who might have challenged him for power.

To take Shyra as his own would humiliate Torrak and solidify V-Kar's dominance.

The Humiliation Of Torrak

The announcement was made before the entire band. V-Kar stood tall, his golden eyes gleaming as he addressed his followers.

"Shyra," he said, his voice sharp and commanding, "will stand at my side. She is mine now."

The reaction was immediate. The band murmured uneasily, their eyes flicking between V-Kar and Torrak. The tension in the air was palpable, the scent of anger and humiliation thick.

Torrak stepped forward, his tail lashing behind him. His eyes burned with fury, his claws flexing. "You would take what is mine?" he growled, his voice trembling with barely restrained rage.

V-Kar's gaze was cold. "You are nothing, Torrak. She was never yours. She was waiting for something greater."

The words were a calculated dagger, and Torrak could not contain his outrage. He lunged at V-Kar, his claws aiming for the throat.

V-Kar moved with the precision of a predator, sidestepping Torrak's attack with ease. The two clashed in the center of the cave, their snarls and roars echoing off the stone walls.

The fight was brutal but brief. Torrak's rage made him reckless, while V-Kar's cold calculation gave him the edge. With a powerful swipe of his claws, V-Kar struck Torrak's face, sending him sprawling to the ground.

As Torrak tried to rise, V-Kar pinned him with a crushing blow, his claws sinking into Torrak's shoulders.

"You dare challenge me?" V-Kar hissed, his voice venomous. "Let this be a lesson to all who think they can defy me."

V-KAR'S EPIC

Without hesitation, V-Kar brought his claws down, ripping into Torrak's face. The other followers watched in horrified silence as V-Kar blinded him, his claws removing the eyes with precise brutality. Torrak's screams echoed through the cave, but they were silenced when V-Kar tore out his tongue with a savage twist of his claws.

Torrak The Reminder
Torrak was not killed. Instead, V-Kar forced him to live, a broken, sightless, and mute shadow of his former self.

He was kept in the cave, a living reminder of V-Kar's power. The others avoided him, their fear of V-Kar deepening as they saw what became of those who opposed him.

Torrak's presence served its purpose. The band grew even more loyal, their obedience fueled by the unspoken knowledge of what V-Kar was capable of.

The Offspring
In time, Shyra bore V-Kar's offspring - a clutch of six younglings, their scales glistening like freshly polished stone. V-Kar viewed them not with affection, but as tools.

"These will be our future," he declared to his band. "But only the strongest will lead."

The younglings were kept in isolation, deep within the cave where food was scarce and the darkness unrelenting. V-Kar made no effort to feed them, watching impassively as the weak fell to hunger and desperation.

When only one remained, a male with piercing golden eyes and a powerful frame, V-Kar stepped forward.

"You are worthy," he said simply.

The youngling - V-Karson - stood tall, his body lean but strong, his gaze fierce. He had survived where his siblings had not, and his father's approval burned in his chest like fire.

The Hibernation

With his heir chosen, V-Kar made another announcement to his band. "I will leave you," he said, his voice carrying through the cave. "But not forever. I will sleep, and when I wake, I will return to see what you have built."

He retreated deep into the cave, far from the light of the entrance. There, in a chamber untouched by time, V-Kar entered hibernation, his body growing still, his breaths slowing to a faint whisper.

The band remained silent as their leader disappeared into the shadows.

V-Karson Rises

V-Karson wasted no time assuming control. Where his father ruled through cunning and calculated fear, V-Karson embodied raw brutality. He demanded constant challenges from his followers, engaging in hand-to-hand combat with the largest and strongest among them.

The jungle became his battlefield, the corpses of defeated foes a testament to his strength. He cared little for strategy or secrecy, focusing instead on dominance through physical power.

V-Karson was a tyrant, his reign marked by violence and unrelenting ambition. But even as he reveled in his strength, the glowing symbols on the cave walls whispered of a power greater than muscle - a power his father had wielded with precision.

The young prince's story was just beginning, and the jungle trembled at the promise of what was to come.

Chapter 11: The Weight Of Time

Centuries passed, and the world above the cave changed in ways both profound and chaotic. V-Karson's brutal reign gave rise to a lineage of tyrants, each ruler ascending through bloodshed and fear. Assassination was not only expected but embraced - a means of proving strength and cunning. To survive, each successor had to be more ruthless than the last.

The descendants of V-Kar carved out a kingdom from the jungle, their power visible in the massive temples that dotted the landscape. These structures, built from enormous stone blocks, were feats of engineering achieved by enslaving the largest dinosaurs. Titans like argentinosauruses were chained and goaded, much like Humans would one day use elephants and oxen. These beasts dragged the stones over vast distances, their sheer power matched only by the cruelty of their handlers.

The temples stood as monuments to fear and dominance, their towering spires scraping the sky, their walls adorned with symbols that had long since lost their meaning.

Religions Born And Forgotten

With power came belief, and with belief came religion. V-Kar's lineage encouraged it, knowing the value of faith in controlling the masses. Priests and prophets rose, each claiming divine favor, their predictions shaping the fears and hopes of the lizardkin.

Some claimed to see the future in the stars, mapping constellations and tracing their movements across the heavens. Others turned to dice and cards, trusting in chance to reveal destiny. The symbols of the caves, once sacred, became tools for divination, their meanings twisted and reimagined with each generation.

But as predictions failed and prophecies went unfulfilled, faith waned, and new religions replaced the old. The cycle repeated endlessly, each belief system burning brightly before collapsing under the weight of its own false promises.

The Star-Ground Heretic

Among these prophets was one who stood apart - not for their charisma, but for their perceived madness. Known as Krelith the Heretic, they rejected the teachings of the temples and instead sought truth in the stars and the ground.

Krelith believed the heavens and the earth were connected, their fates intertwined. They spent their days studying the patterns of the stars and the strata of the ground, combining the two into a strange, fractured science.

From their studies, Krelith arrived at a shocking conclusion: a massive rock from the sky would one day obliterate the world as they knew it.

"Look to the heavens!" they cried, their voice echoing through the temples. "The stars whisper of our doom! The ground trembles with its coming!"

The lizardkin laughed. To them, Krelith was a fool, a mad creature chasing shadows. Even the priests dismissed the heretic's warnings, seeing them as a threat to the established order.

But Krelith persisted, their voice growing hoarse as they begged others to listen.

The Unheeded Warning

One night, the stars began to change. A bright light appeared in the sky, growing larger with each passing day. Krelith's cries grew frantic, their predictions becoming more specific.

"The rock comes!" they shouted. "It will strike with the force of a thousand storms! Everything will burn!"

Still, no one listened. The rulers of the temples dismissed the light as a passing phenomenon, their attention focused on maintaining their grip on power.

By the time the truth became undeniable, it was too late.

The Awakening Of V-Kar

Deep within the cave, V-Kar stirred. The tremors from the approaching impact reached even the lowest depths, faint but insistent. His slumber had lasted centuries, but now the world called to him again.

Rising slowly, V-Kar stretched his massive frame, his claws scraping against the stone. His golden eyes glinted in the dim light of the cave, their sharpness undulled by time.

V-KAR'S EPIC

He moved to the edge of the slumbering chamber, where a handful of chosen followers waited. These were the strongest and most loyal of his bloodline, selected to join him in the depths.

"The world grows restless," V-Kar said, his voice low and steady. "We will wait here until it is ready again."

Without another word, he led the chosen deeper into the cave, descending into chambers untouched by light. Here, the air was colder, the stone walls smooth and unbroken.

V-Kar entered a new slumber, his body coiling into stillness, his followers settling around him. The symbols on the walls glowed faintly, their light casting shadows that flickered like distant memories.

The Impact

Above, the rock struck.

The impact was catastrophic, a force unlike anything the lizardkin had ever known. The ground heaved and cracked, firestorms swept the land, and ash darkened the skies. The temples crumbled, their towering spires collapsing under the weight of the tremors.

The dinosaurs that had labored to build the monuments vanished, their massive forms no match for the cataclysm. The lizardkin, scattered and disorganized, fell into chaos.

Krelith's warnings echoed in the minds of the survivors, their laughter now replaced with regret. But the heretic's voice was silent, lost in the devastation.

V-KAR'S EPIC

<u>The Silence Of The Deep</u>

In the depths of the cave, V-Kar and his chosen remained untouched. The cataclysm could not reach them, its fury muffled by the stone.

Centuries passed as the surface healed, new life rising from the ashes of the old. The temples became ruins, their symbols eroded by time, their purpose forgotten.

But V-Kar slept on, his golden eyes closed, his mind undisturbed. He would wake again when the world was ready - when his time would come once more.

Chapter 12: The Early Awakening

The silence of the cave was broken by a faint, rhythmic tremor. Deep in the hibernation chamber, one of V-Kar's chosen stirred. His golden eyes opened slowly, reflecting the faint glow of the symbols on the walls.

Karos, one of the eldest and most loyal of V-Kar's followers, rose from his coiled position. Around him, the others slept in their stony alcoves, their bodies still and cold. But Karos felt the pull of the world above, an instinctive urge to explore what lay beyond the cave's depths.

Another followed: Syrris, a sharp-witted female with a keen sense of curiosity. Together, they moved toward the surface, their claws clicking softly against the stone as they ascended through the winding tunnels.

When they reached the cave's mouth, the sight that greeted them was both awe-inspiring and desolate.

A New World

The surface was unrecognizable. The lush jungles and towering ferns that had once defined their world were gone, replaced by sparse, rough foliage clinging to rocky soil. The air was cooler, carrying the faint scent of ash mixed with the sharp tang of new growth.

Small mammals darted through the underbrush, their furred bodies an odd contrast to the scaly creatures Karos and Syrris had known. Insects buzzed in abundance, their presence a constant hum in the stillness.

The vast beasts of old - the dinosaurs that had been both ally and foe - were nowhere to be seen. In their place were smaller reptiles, scurrying lizards with quick, nervous movements.

Karos crouched, his claws brushing the soil. "The world has changed," he said, his voice low and measured. "It is no longer ours."

Syrris scanned the horizon, her tail flicking thoughtfully. "The surface will heal," she said. "But it is not ready yet. We cannot thrive here."

The Return Underground

They spent days exploring, their movements cautious and deliberate. They ventured to the remains of the once-great temples, finding only crumbled stone and overgrown ruins. The symbols that had once adorned the walls were now faint scratches, their meaning long eroded by time.

The oceans, however, teemed with life. Fish of every shape and size darted through crystal-clear waters, their movements a reminder that life had not been extinguished, only altered.

When Karos and Syrris returned to the cave, they brought news to the few others who had begun to stir. Together, they made a decision: they would not wait passively for the surface to heal. They would rebuild underground, preparing for the day when their kind could reclaim the world above.

V-KAR'S EPIC

Building The Metropolis
The task was monumental, but the determination of V-Kar's chosen was unshakable. They expanded the cave, carving tunnels and chambers deep into the earth. Using the remnants of their knowledge and ingenuity, they began to craft a new society, one that thrived in the darkness.

Their first breakthrough came with metallurgy. By mining the rich veins of ore buried within the earth, they forged tools and weapons stronger than anything they had known before. Bronze and iron became the backbone of their civilization, their creations gleaming even in the dim light of their underground world.

Next came bio-engineering. Observing the small creatures that survived above and below ground, they began experimenting, selectively breeding lizards and insects to create new forms of life. They engineered creatures that could serve as beasts of burden, hunters, and even sources of light, their bioluminescent bodies casting an eerie glow in the darkened chambers.

A Flourishing Underground World
Centuries passed, and the lizardkin metropolis flourished. Vast underground halls were adorned with intricate carvings, their walls telling the story of their survival and transformation. Rivers of molten metal flowed through forges, while carefully cultivated fungal gardens provided sustenance.

They built machines powered by heat and pressure, their technology advancing in ways their ancestors could never have imagined. Yet, through it all, they never forgot their purpose: to wait for the return of V-Kar, the mage-leader whose fire had inspired them to survive.

His name became legend, spoken with reverence and fear. Priests chanted his teachings, their voices echoing through the halls. The symbols of the cave were studied obsessively, their meanings reinterpreted and expanded.

The Awakening Of V-Kar

When the time came, the earth trembled faintly, a ripple that passed through the metropolis like an unspoken signal. In the deepest chamber, V-Kar's golden eyes opened.

He rose slowly, his movements deliberate, his body coiled with the power of centuries of rest. Around him, the chosen who had remained by his side stirred, their breaths quickening as they sensed his awakening.

V-Kar stepped forward, his claws clicking against the stone. The symbols on the walls glowed brighter, their light reflecting in his sharp gaze.

When he emerged into the metropolis, the lizardkin fell silent. Hundreds of eyes turned to him, their awe palpable. The air was thick with the metallic tang of molten metal, the earthy scent of the fungal gardens, and the faint musk of the engineered beasts that roamed the halls.

V-Kar stood tall, his presence commanding. His gaze swept over the thriving city, taking in its scale and complexity.

"You have done well," he said, his voice low but resonant. "You have waited. You have endured. Now, we will rise."

The Promise Of The Future

The lizardkin erupted into cheers, their voices reverberating through the underground chambers. V-Kar raised a claw, silencing them with a single gesture.

"The surface is ours to reclaim," he said. "But we will not rush. We will move with purpose, with strength, and with the fire that has always guided us."

The metropolis buzzed with renewed energy, its people driven by the promise of their leader's return.

But V-Kar's gaze turned inward, his mind racing with plans. The surface was not just a place to rebuild - it was a place to conquer. And the lizardkin would not simply survive; they would dominate.

Chapter 13: The Pyramid Of Stars

Centuries passed like whispers on the wind, and the lizardkin civilization evolved under the watchful eye of their kings. V-Kar, their Hegemon, remained in his deep slumber, stirring only every few hundred years to awaken and guide his people with prophetic purpose. Each awakening was marked with reverence, his return seen as divine intervention.

During his most recent emergence, V-Kar selected a new king, Rhazyn, a cunning and disciplined leader. With his chosen ruler in place, V-Kar retreated once more into the depths of the cave, leaving his people to carry out his will.

Rhazyn, driven by the need to protect their Hegemon's resting place, ordered the construction of a great pyramid.

The Great Pyramid

The pyramid rose slowly above the lizardkin metropolis, its construction a testament to their strength and ingenuity. Each block was immense, hauled from the surrounding mountains and dragged into place by the massive beasts they had domesticated. Elephants, bred for their sheer power, pulled the stone blocks across the land with thick ropes and wooden sledges.

The structure became a marvel of engineering. Its outer surface gleamed with polished limestone that reflected the sun, while its interior was a labyrinth of secret passageways and hidden chambers.

V-KAR'S EPIC

The pyramid served dual purposes: it was both a monument to V-Kar's might and a safeguard for his hibernation chambers. Only the highest-ranking lizardkin knew of the concealed entrances leading to the Hegemon's resting place. Traps and false passages were designed to deter intruders, while priests and guards patrolled its halls, their loyalty unwavering.

A Society Of Combat

Over the centuries, the lizardkin grew increasingly martial. Their society became centered around combat, with every citizen trained in the arts of war. Swords, spears, and shields forged in their underground forges were carried with pride, each warrior honing their skills in duels and group battles.

Though the lizardkin excelled in combat, their scientific advancements were limited. Only a few dedicated themselves to pursuits beyond war. Those who did focused mainly on the study of the stars.

The Religion Of The Stars

The sky above the pyramid became the lizardkin's new scripture. They observed the heavens with awe, charting the movements of the stars and constellations. Their priests identified two groups of stars - lines of celestial bodies that traveled faster than others and repeated their patterns over centuries and millennia.

These stars became sacred, their movements interpreted as signs from the heavens. The priests believed that the stars reflected the will of their Hegemon, and their alignment was seen as an omen of V-Kar's next awakening.

Rituals were performed beneath the open sky, with offerings and dances timed to the movements of the constellations. The lizardkin's astrology became a deeply ingrained part of their culture, guiding decisions on war, construction, and leadership.

The Rise Of Husbandry

While combat dominated their lives, the lizardkin also developed skills in animal husbandry. They bred the local mammals, creating beasts suited for labor, food, and even companionship. Their efforts were meticulous, guided by the same discipline they applied to their martial training.

Over generations, they transformed the small, skittish creatures of the post-impact world into useful and hardy animals. This practice not only strengthened their society but also allowed them to expand their influence over the surrounding lands.

But one day, their carefully laid traps were sprung by something unexpected.

A New Mammal

The hunters returned from the forest with strange news. They had found signs of a new mammal - one that had eluded their traps and evaded capture.

"This one is different," said Wigwas, one of the hunters, her voice tinged with both curiosity and frustration. "It walks upright, like us. It is cunning, breaking free from our snares and avoiding our trails."

The priests dismissed the reports at first, believing them to be exaggerations. But as more hunters returned with similar stories, the truth became undeniable. This creature, whatever it was, did not behave like the other mammals they had encountered.

"The stars have foretold this," murmured Kaerik, one of the high priests, his gaze fixed on the night sky. "A challenger has arisen from the earth, one unlike any we have faced before."

Rhazyn, ever cautious, ordered his best hunters to track the creature. They laid more traps, carefully hidden, and waited. Days turned into weeks, but the creature remained elusive.

The Hominid

One night, under the glow of the sacred stars, a group of hunters spotted it for the first time. It moved through the forest on two legs, its gait strange and awkward compared to the smooth movements of the lizardkin. Its body was covered in rough hair, and its face was flat, its features expressive in ways the lizardkin found alien.

The creature paused, sniffing the air, its eyes scanning the shadows. Then, as if sensing the hunters' presence, it fled, vanishing into the underbrush with surprising speed.

The hunters returned to the pyramid with their report, their expressions uneasy.

"It is clever," Wigwas said, her claws gripping her spear tightly. "More clever than any prey we have hunted before."

Rhazyn listened carefully, his mind racing. The emergence of this new creature posed a question he could not yet answer: was it a threat to be eradicated, or a curiosity to be studied?

The Watchful King

Rhazyn ordered the priests to consult the stars, hoping for guidance. Meanwhile, he instructed the hunters to continue their pursuit, urging them to capture the creature alive if possible.

But as the lizardkin pondered the implications of this new arrival, the Hegemon slept on, deep in his hidden chambers beneath the pyramid.

The question lingered in the minds of the lizardkin as they looked to the heavens, their gaze drawn to the sacred constellations that had shaped their destiny. What role would this creature play in their future?

The answer, they knew, would come in time. And when it did, their Hegemon would awaken to lead them once more.

Chapter 14: The Elusive Prey

The forest surrounding the great pyramid buzzed with activity as the lizardkin hunters spread out, their movements silent and methodical. Traps were set with precision: snares hidden beneath leaves, pits dug into the soft soil, and nets woven so fine they could hold even the smallest of creatures.

Yet the elusive upright mammal continued to evade them.

Wigwas crouched by a broken snare, her sharp eyes scanning the area. The rope had been cut cleanly, the edges frayed as though the creature had worked it apart with nimble fingers. Nearby, faint tracks led away, their shape strange - broad, flat feet with no claws to mark the earth.

"It's not just clever," Wigwas murmured. "It's learning."

Behind her, the other hunters exchanged uneasy glances. Their prey was no ordinary beast, and its ability to adapt made it dangerous in ways they had not anticipated.

The Hominid's Tricks

For weeks, the hunters pursued the creature, but every attempt to capture it ended in failure. The traps were avoided or dismantled, the trails obscured by cleverly placed debris. Sometimes, the hunters found signs of the creature watching them: a faint scent in the air, the rustle of leaves just out of sight.

"It knows we're here," Wigwas told Rhazyn during her report. "It's toying with us."

Rhazyn's jaw tightened, his golden eyes narrowing. "Then we must stop toying with it. Double the traps. Use the venom nets."

The venom nets were one of the lizardkin's more ingenious inventions: fine strands coated in the sap of a poisonous plant that numbed anything it touched. To the hunters, it was a weapon of last resort - dangerous to handle, but effective.

The nets were laid across key pathways, hidden beneath layers of foliage. Days later, one of the nets was found torn to shreds, its strands burned by the acid-like saliva of the local insects, which the hominid had somehow weaponized against it.

The hunters returned to Rhazyn in frustration.

"This creature…" Wigwas began, hesitating. "It's not prey. It's something else entirely."

The Priests' Interpretation

As the hunters struggled, the priests of the pyramid gathered beneath the open sky to consult the stars. Their eyes, sharp and gleaming, traced the sacred constellations that had guided their civilization for centuries.

Kaerik, the high priest, stood at the center of the gathering, his claws clasped tightly around a polished orb that reflected the heavens. "The stars are restless," he intoned. "The arrival of this creature is not an accident. It is a sign."

The gathered priests murmured among themselves, their voices rising like the hiss of steam.

Kaerik continued, his voice growing louder. "The creature comes from the stars themselves! Its path mirrors the movement of the sacred constellations - the fast stars that lead us through the ages."

A younger priest stepped forward, her eyes wide with awe. "Do you believe it is a messenger, High One? Sent to test us?"

Kaerik's expression darkened. "Messenger or invader, the stars do not speak of peace. They speak of fire and chaos. This creature brings disruption, and we must prepare."

The priests debated late into the night, their discussions ranging from prophecy to strategy. Some argued for immediate action, calling for the hunters to redouble their efforts and bring the creature to the pyramid for study. Others urged caution, warning that provoking it could lead to unforeseen consequences.

In the end, Kaerik made the decision. "We must capture it alive," he declared. "Its purpose must be revealed before we decide its fate."

The Hunters' Last Attempt
Under Rhazyn's orders, the hunters launched a final, coordinated effort to capture the creature. Dozens of traps were laid, the venom nets reinforced with stronger materials, and the most experienced trackers joined the pursuit.

The forest became a battlefield of wits, the hunters moving with precision, their every step calculated. For days, they followed the faint traces of the creature: the bent grass where it had crouched, the discarded shells of small fruits it had eaten, the faint scent of its hair carried on the wind.

Finally, they cornered it in a narrow ravine, its escape routes cut off by the steep rock walls. Wigwas stepped forward, her spear raised, her voice steady.

"You have nowhere to run," she said. "Surrender."

The creature turned to face her. It was small, its limbs thin but strong, its flat face expressive. Its dark eyes gleamed with intelligence, scanning the hunters with a mixture of fear and defiance.

Wigwas hesitated. For the first time, she felt a flicker of doubt. This was no mindless beast. There was something unsettlingly familiar in its gaze.

Before she could act, the creature let out a strange, guttural cry and hurled a rock at her feet. The ground exploded in a burst of smoke and sparks, a trick the hunters could not have anticipated.

When the smoke cleared, the creature was gone.

The King's Frustration

Rhazyn's claws scraped against the stone throne as he listened to the hunters' report. His golden eyes burned with frustration.

"You failed," he said, his voice cold.

"It outwitted us," Wigwas admitted, her gaze downcast. "This creature is unlike anything we have encountered."

"It is an affront to the Hegemon's will," Rhazyn growled. "We must not allow it to defy us."

Kaerik, standing nearby, placed a clawed hand on the king's shoulder. "Patience, my king. The stars tell us that all things come in their time. If this creature eludes us now, it is because the heavens have not yet revealed its purpose."

Rhazyn's tail lashed, but he said nothing. The priests' influence was too strong to ignore, and their words carried weight even in matters of the hunt.

A New Mystery

As the hunters returned to the pyramid to regroup, the creature's presence lingered in their minds. It had eluded capture, but its actions raised questions none could answer.

Why had it resisted so fiercely? What drove it to evade them? And most importantly, where had it come from?

The priests continued their studies of the stars, searching for clues, while the hunters prepared for another pursuit. But even as the lizardkin planned their next steps, the creature watched them from the shadows, its mind working as quickly as theirs.

V-KAR'S EPIC

In the stillness of the forest, beneath the eternal dance of the constellations, the stage was set for a confrontation that would shape the future of both species.

Chapter 15: The Clever Opponent

The lizardkin's society thrived beneath the towering pyramid and within the sprawling underground metropolis. Their civilization, disciplined and battle-hardened, had never faced a true challenge in centuries. The mammalian intruders, once dismissed as minor nuisances, were proving to be something far more formidable.

What began as a single elusive hominid sighting had turned into an ongoing battle against a growing, adaptable foe. These creatures were unlike anything the lizardkin had encountered. Their cleverness, rapid reproduction, and ability to cooperate in large packs turned them into an ever-increasing problem that no spear or trap could fully contain.

The First Victory

Under Rhazyn's orders, a new hunting party was formed, larger and better equipped. The priests had blessed their weapons, chanting beneath the open sky to invoke the power of the sacred stars. The hunters moved with precision, using coordinated ambush tactics perfected over generations of combat.

Their target was a small group of hominids that had been raiding the outskirts of the forest near the pyramid. The hunters surrounded them in a clearing, cutting off every escape route.

The battle was swift and brutal. Though the hominids fought fiercely, using sharpened stones and wooden clubs, they were no match for the lizardkin's superior weapons and discipline. When it was over, the hunters returned to the pyramid with trophies: the broken weapons of the hominids and the bodies of their fallen.

For a moment, the lizardkin believed they had asserted their dominance. But the victory was short-lived.

A Growing Threat

Within weeks, reports began pouring in from the outer patrols. The hominids were adapting. They avoided the traps, broke into supply caches, and attacked isolated groups of lizardkin with surprising coordination.

"They're learning," Wigwas told Rhazyn during a council meeting. "Each time we strike them, they come back stronger. They've started working together in larger groups, and their numbers are growing faster than we can track."

Rhazyn's claws drummed against the stone table. "Their reproduction is their advantage," he growled. "They breed faster than we can kill them."

Kaerik, the high priest, interjected. "The stars have warned us of this. The cycle repeats itself. Their strength lies in numbers, yes, but also in their ability to adapt. We must look to the heavens for guidance, as we always have."

Rhazyn scowled but nodded. He could not afford to alienate the priests, whose influence kept the population unified.

V-KAR'S EPIC

The Ambush At River's Edge

The lizardkin prepared for another major offensive. Scouts had identified a large group of hominids gathering near the river, where the creatures seemed to be building primitive shelters from branches and mud.

Rhazyn himself led the hunting party, determined to deliver a decisive blow. The lizardkin attacked at dawn, descending on the hominids with practiced efficiency.

At first, it seemed like another victory. The lizardkin cut through the shelters, driving the hominids into disarray. But then the tide turned. From the riverbank, more hominids emerged - dozens more than the scouts had reported.

The lizardkin were overwhelmed. The hominids attacked with sharpened spears and stones, their coordination unexpected and devastating. Rhazyn barely managed to rally his forces, retreating with heavy losses.

The survivors returned to the pyramid in silence, their pride shattered.

Fractures In The Society

The defeats began to wear on the lizardkin. For centuries, their society had been built on the belief in their inherent superiority, their discipline, and the prophetic guidance of their Hegemon. Now, cracks began to form.

Whispers spread through the underground city. Some questioned Rhazyn's leadership, while others doubted the priests' interpretations of the stars.

Wigwas voiced her frustration during a council meeting. "We cannot rely on prophecies alone. We need strategy. These creatures are not beasts; they are something else entirely. If we don't adapt, we will lose everything."

Kaerik's eyes narrowed. "The stars have guided us through countless trials. Do not presume to doubt their wisdom."

"And yet the stars haven't stopped the hominids," Wigwas retorted, earning a sharp glare from the priests.

Rhazyn raised a claw, silencing the argument. "Enough. We will find a way to turn this tide. The Hegemon chose me to lead, and I will not fail."

The Hominids' Resilience

The hominids continued to evolve. Their tools became more advanced, their traps more cunning. They worked together in larger groups, their communication primitive but effective.

The lizardkin won a few victories, but each success came at a greater cost. For every group of hominids they killed, twice as many seemed to emerge.

The priests held ceremonies to renew faith in the Hegemon, urging the lizardkin to trust in the stars. But the hunters grew weary, their morale faltering. The hominids had become more than a threat - they were an existential challenge.

A Desperate Decision

In a private meeting, Rhazyn called upon Kaerik and Wigwas. The king's expression was grim, his claws tapping rhythmically against the stone table.

"We cannot keep fighting them like this," he said. "Their numbers will overwhelm us. We need a new approach."

Kaerik nodded slowly. "The stars suggest that this is a trial of patience. Perhaps we should fortify our defenses, retreating underground until the surface is ours to reclaim."

Wigwas, ever the pragmatist, shook her head. "Retreat is surrender. We need to outthink them. Find their weaknesses. They're clever, yes, but they're also fragile. We've seen how quickly they fall to disease and hunger. If we can cut off their resources, we might stand a chance."

Rhazyn considered their words carefully. "We will do both," he decided. "We will strengthen our defenses while finding ways to exploit their weaknesses. The Hegemon chose me for a reason, and I will not let him wake to a world ruled by these creatures."

The Balance Of Power

The lizardkin began fortifying their underground city, reinforcing the pyramid's secret entrances and expanding their network of tunnels. At the same time, they launched targeted raids against the hominids, destroying their food stores and water supplies.

The battles raged on, each side adapting, each side determined. The lizardkin's martial discipline and cunning clashed with the hominids' resilience and ingenuity.

But even as the struggle continued, the stars above turned slowly, their patterns unchanged. And deep within the earth, V-Kar slept on, his golden eyes closed, his body coiled in stillness.

The question lingered in the minds of the lizardkin: would their Hegemon wake to lead them to victory, or would the world above become forever lost to the rising tide of the mammalian invaders?

Chapter 16: The Retreat Underground

The battles with the hominids had reached a grim conclusion: the lizardkin could not win. The surface, once their hunting ground and place of dominance, had become a hostile land ruled by cunning, rapidly reproducing packs of mammalian intruders.

King Rhazyn called for a retreat. The lizardkin descended into their subterranean metropolis, leaving the surface world to the creatures that now roamed it freely. The great pyramid, with its gleaming limestone walls, stood as a lonely sentinel above, its hidden entrances sealed to protect the Hegemon's resting place below.

A New Focus

Within the dark chambers of their underground city, the lizardkin turned their attention inward. If they could not outmatch the hominids in numbers or adaptability, they would craft their advantage through other means. Their society began to shift, prioritizing breeding programs to enhance specific traits within their population.

The priests proclaimed this effort sacred, framing it as a divine mission guided by the stars. Every decision, every pairing was calculated and approved under their watchful eyes. To the lizardkin, this was no mere science - it was prophecy fulfilled through flesh and blood.

V-KAR'S EPIC

The Breeding Programs

Some lizardkin were selected for their immense size and physical power. These individuals were paired repeatedly, their offspring towering over their kin. These "Titans," as they were called, became symbols of brute force, capable of breaking stone with their claws and dragging immense loads through the underground tunnels.

The Titans were used to expand the city's depths, carving out new chambers and fortifications. Though their intelligence was often lacking, their sheer strength made them invaluable.

Another group was bred for toxicity. Drawing inspiration from the venomous creatures of the surface, the lizardkin developed a lineage with natural venom glands. These "Venomous Elite" could produce poisons in their claws and saliva, making them deadly in combat.

The priests often viewed the Venomous Elite with a mix of awe and fear, their deadly potential seen as both a gift and a curse.

Aggression was the hallmark of the third program. These lizardkin were bred for their fiery tempers and relentless drive in battle. Known as "Berserkers," they were unpredictable and dangerous, even to their own kind.

Kept in isolation when not in combat, the Berserkers were seen as weapons to be unleashed only in the most dire of circumstances.

V-KAR'S EPIC

The Role Of Scientists

While the breeding programs flourished, the lizardkin remained wary of those among them who pursued knowledge beyond the stars and combat. Scientists were seen as a necessary evil - tolerated but shunned by the larger population.

These individuals, often working in secrecy, were responsible for breakthroughs that enhanced the breeding programs. They studied anatomy, toxins, and genetics, their work advancing the lizardkin's understanding of their own biology.

One such scientist, Drakess, worked tirelessly in the shadow of the pyramid's lower chambers. His discoveries in selective breeding and toxin refinement were unparalleled, but his presence made others uneasy.

"You twist the sacred," one priest told him, their voice laced with disdain. "Your methods are unnatural."

Drakess's reply was calm but firm. "Survival is not natural. It is earned."

Despite the priests' disapproval, Drakess's work was allowed to continue, his contributions too valuable to ignore.

A Society Of Fear And Purpose

The lizardkin's retreat underground did not weaken their resolve. If anything, it made them more focused. Their society, already built on discipline and fear, grew even more insular and rigid.

Every citizen had a role to play, whether as a warrior, breeder, or laborer. The priests maintained their influence, interpreting the stars and guiding the population with prophecies that justified their actions.

But cracks began to form in their unity. The Berserkers were unpredictable, their aggression sometimes spilling over into the city's populace. The Venomous Elite, while powerful, were seen as unclean, their toxic nature separating them from the rest of society.

And the scientists, always working in the shadows, were a constant source of unease.

The Weight Of Waiting

Years turned into decades, and decades into centuries. The lizardkin waited, their underground city growing larger and more intricate. They rarely ventured to the surface, except to scout or gather resources. The hominids above had thrived, their numbers swelling, their tools and strategies becoming more advanced.

King Rhazyn, now aged and weary, addressed his people one final time. "We have done what we must to survive," he said. "The Hegemon will wake again, and when he does, he will see the strength we have built."

As Rhazyn's reign came to an end, the lizardkin continued their sacred work, their eyes ever turned to the heavens - visible only through the small, concealed openings at the pyramid's peak.

<u>A Distant Hope</u>

In the deepest chamber of the pyramid, V-Kar slept on, undisturbed by the passage of time. His golden eyes remained closed, his body coiled in stillness.

But the symbols on the walls seemed to glow faintly, their light pulsing like a heartbeat. The lizardkin's faith in their Hegemon never wavered, even as the world above grew ever more distant.

They believed, as they always had, that V-Kar's awakening would signal their return to greatness. Until then, they would prepare, their society sharpening itself like a blade, ready for the moment when their time would come again.

Chapter 17: Fissures Beneath The Surface

The underground metropolis of the lizardkin was a marvel of resilience, discipline, and ingenuity, but centuries of isolation and specialization had begun to take their toll. The once-unified society, bound together by the memory of V-Kar and the authority of the priests, was now plagued by fractures.

The strict caste system created by the breeding programs fostered tension between the groups. The Titans, with their massive strength, resented the priests and scientists who dictated their work. The Venomous Elite, feared for their toxicity, found themselves isolated even as they were celebrated for their power. The Berserkers, unpredictable and dangerous, were kept in chains for the safety of others, their fury simmering beneath the surface.

The Titans' Resentment

Deep in the forges, where molten metal flowed like rivers, the Titans toiled endlessly. Their size and strength made them indispensable in the construction of new chambers and the maintenance of the city's defenses. But their simple minds and straightforward nature left them vulnerable to manipulation.

Among them, a Titan named Nimatowin began to voice his frustration. "Why do we obey the small ones?" he rumbled, his voice echoing through the cavernous forge. "We build the city, we dig the tunnels, but they call us brutes and keep us below them."

His words spread like wildfire among the Titans, planting seeds of dissent. The priests, always watchful, sensed the growing unrest and sought to quell it with promises of divine purpose.

"You are the foundation of our society," one priest told Nimatowin. "Without you, we could not thrive. The stars have chosen you for this sacred role."

But the words rang hollow. Nimatowin and his kin continued to grumble, their discontent simmering just beneath the surface.

The Venomous Elite's Isolation

The Venomous Elite, while respected for their power, were viewed with suspicion by the rest of the population. Their toxic nature made them dangerous even in peaceful settings, and their venomous touch was seen as both a blessing and a curse.

One Venomous warrior, Kwekwe, had grown weary of her isolation. She approached the priests with a simple question: "Why do we fight for a society that fears us?"

The priests responded with carefully chosen words. "You are the guardians of our people," they said. "Your power protects us all. It is a burden, yes, but also an honor."

But Kwekwe was not satisfied. She began to wonder if the Venomous Elite might find greater purpose on their own, away from those who shunned them.

V-KAR'S EPIC

The Berserkers' Rage

The Berserkers, bred for aggression, were a constant source of unease. They were kept under strict control, their chambers isolated from the rest of the city. But even chains could not hold their fury forever.

One Berserker, Akuaq, managed to break free during a training session. His rampage left three Titans dead and several chambers damaged before he was subdued.

The incident shook the city, raising questions about the wisdom of keeping such dangerous creatures within their walls.

"We cannot control them," Wigwas told the council. "They are a weapon that will destroy us if we are not careful."

But the priests refused to abandon the Berserkers, claiming that their rage would be needed when the Hegemon returned.

The Surface Expeditions

While tensions brewed below, the need for resources forced the lizardkin to make rare and dangerous expeditions to the surface. These missions, led by skilled scouts, were fraught with peril.

The hominids above had continued to evolve, their tools and strategies growing ever more advanced. Their settlements had expanded, and their numbers now dwarfed those of the lizardkin.

One expedition, led by Wigwas herself, ventured to the ruins of an old temple. The surface air was crisp and cool, the scent of damp earth mingling with the faint musk of animals.

Wigwas crouched in the shadows, her golden eyes scanning the area. The ruins were overgrown with vines, but the stone blocks were still intact - a testament to the lizardkin's engineering.

She signaled her team to move forward, their movements silent and deliberate. They gathered what they could: fragments of stone carvings, shards of ancient tools, and a few scattered bones.

But as they prepared to leave, they heard the sound of footsteps - many footsteps.

A Close Encounter

The hominids had found them. A group of them emerged from the trees, their bodies covered in fur-lined hides, their hands gripping sharpened spears.

Wigwas's team froze, their claws flexing as they prepared for a fight. But the hominids didn't attack immediately. They seemed cautious, their eyes scanning the lizardkin with curiosity and wariness.

"They've grown smarter," Wigwas whispered to one of her scouts. "They're studying us."

The standoff lasted only moments before the hominids charged. The lizardkin fought fiercely, their venom-tipped weapons cutting through the attackers with precision. But the hominids' sheer numbers and coordination overwhelmed them.

Wigwas barely managed to escape, retreating with only two survivors.

The Lessons Of Defeat
When Wigwas returned to the underground city, she reported the expedition's failure to Rhazyn and the council.

"They are no longer just prey," she said. "They are hunters. They plan, they adapt, and they outnumber us."

Rhazyn's expression darkened. "Then we must adapt as well," he said. "The surface may no longer be ours, but we cannot allow them to grow unchecked."

A Fractured Society
The tensions within the city grew worse as news of the expedition's failure spread. The Titans grumbled that they were being worked to death for a society that could not even protect its own. The Venomous Elite whispered of abandoning the city altogether, seeking a place where their power would be respected. The Berserkers, restless and unpredictable, became even harder to control.

And through it all, the priests continued to preach the will of the stars, urging unity and patience. "The Hegemon will awaken," they said. "And he will lead us to reclaim what is ours."

But as the lizardkin looked to the surface, where the hominids continued to thrive, doubt began to creep into their hearts.

Chapter 18: Splintering Foundations

The underground city, once a testament to the lizardkin's resilience and discipline, teetered on the edge of chaos. Centuries of isolation, compounded by the growing threat of the hominids above, had strained the delicate balance of their society. The fractures that had been forming for generations now widened, threatening to tear them apart.

The Titans' Revolt

The Titans, overworked and underappreciated, finally reached their breaking point. Nimatowin, emboldened by years of resentment, rallied his fellow Titans in the forges. His massive frame towered over the smaller lizardkin as he addressed them, his voice booming through the chamber.

"We build their walls, dig their tunnels, and carry their burdens!" he roared, his claws slamming into the stone floor. "Yet they call us brutes and leave us in the dark. No more! We are the foundation of this city, and it is time they remember that!"

The Titans' rebellion began with sabotage. They slowed the construction of new chambers, withheld their labor, and spread discontent among the lower castes. The priests, alarmed by the growing unrest, sent emissaries to negotiate, but Nimatowin dismissed them with scorn.

"If they want our strength," he said, "they will pay for it in respect."

The Venomous Elite's Defiance

Meanwhile, the Venomous Elite, led by Kwekwe, began to withdraw from the rest of society. Their isolation, once enforced by fear, became a choice. They retreated to the outermost chambers of the city, where they established their own enclave.

Kwekwe's vision was clear: "If they fear us, let them stay away. We will build our own future, one where our power is not seen as a curse."

The priests sent envoys to persuade the Venomous Elite to return, but Kwekwe refused. "We fight their battles and protect their lives, yet they treat us like poison," she said. "We owe them nothing."

Her defiance inspired others, and soon, smaller groups of discontented lizardkin began joining the Venomous enclave.

The Berserkers' Breaking Point

The Berserkers, always a volatile element, became even more unpredictable. Akuaq, the Berserker who had broken free during the earlier rampage, became a symbol of their uncontrollable nature.

Confined to their chambers, the Berserkers grew restless. Their handlers, already stretched thin, struggled to maintain control. When a poorly planned training session ended in another deadly outburst, the council was forced to consider drastic measures.

"We cannot keep them here," Wigwas argued during a council meeting. "They are a danger to us all."

"But they are our greatest weapon," Kaerik countered. "When the Hegemon awakens, they will be his army."

The debate ended with no resolution, leaving the Berserkers to stew in their rage.

Plans Against The Hominids

Amid the internal strife, Rhazyn worked to address the growing threat of the hominids. The recent expedition's failure had made it clear that the lizardkin's traditional tactics were no longer sufficient.

"We cannot fight them on their terms," he told the council. "They are too numerous, too resourceful. If we are to succeed, we must think beyond the old ways."

Rhazyn ordered a team of scouts to map the hominids' settlements, studying their behavior and weaknesses. The scouts returned with detailed reports:

Organization: The hominids were forming primitive but effective hierarchies, with leaders directing groups in coordinated efforts.

Settlements: Their villages were expanding, with simple but sturdy structures that provided shelter and storage.

Reproduction: Their numbers continued to grow rapidly, their population outpacing that of the lizardkin.

Rhazyn proposed a plan of targeted sabotage: destroy the hominids' food supplies, contaminate their water sources, and disrupt their settlements through carefully planned raids.

A Dangerous Mission

Wigwas, ever loyal to the cause, volunteered to lead the first mission. Her team, composed of skilled scouts and Venomous warriors, ventured to the surface under cover of darkness.

The mission was fraught with danger. The hominids' patrols were growing more frequent, and their traps were becoming more sophisticated.

As Wigwas's team approached a large settlement, they worked quickly, spreading poison into the nearby river and setting fire to a storage hut filled with food. The flames lit up the night, drawing the attention of the hominids.

The team managed to escape, but not without losses. Two scouts were captured, their cries echoing through the forest as they were dragged away.

When Wigwas returned to the city, she reported the mission's partial success. "We hurt them," she said. "But they are learning, just as we are."

V-KAR'S EPIC

Tensions Boil Over

The success of the sabotage mission did little to ease the tensions within the city. The Titans' rebellion grew bolder, with Nimatowin openly defying the priests. The Venomous Elite continued to expand their enclave, their separation becoming more pronounced. The Berserkers, still confined, grew more dangerous with each passing day.

Kaerik addressed the council, his tone urgent. "The Hegemon must awaken. Only his guidance can unite us and lead us to victory."

But Rhazyn hesitated. "The Hegemon sleeps because the time is not yet right," he said. "If we wake him too soon, we risk failing him."

Wigwas, ever practical, voiced her concerns. "If we wait much longer, there may be no city left for him to lead."

The Looming Crisis

As the lizardkin struggled with their internal divisions and the relentless threat of the hominids, the weight of their situation grew heavier. The stars above, once a source of guidance and hope, now seemed distant and indifferent.

In the deepest chamber of the pyramid, V-Kar slept on, undisturbed by the turmoil above. But the symbols on the walls pulsed faintly, as if sensing the growing need for their Hegemon's return.

V-KAR'S EPIC

The lizardkin faced a choice: continue their descent into division and chaos, or find a way to unite before it was too late.

Chapter 19: The Awakening Looms

The lizardkin's society trembled on the edge of collapse. The once-mighty metropolis that had stood as a bastion of unity and strength was now fractured, each caste retreating into its own purpose or rebellion. All the while, the relentless pressure of the hominids above grew stronger. The priests, ever watchful of the stars, debated the ultimate question: Should the Hegemon, V-Kar, be awakened to save them from ruin?

The Castes' Breaking Point

Nimatowin and his Titans reached their limit. Refusing to work on the city's infrastructure, they barricaded themselves within the forges. Fires burned low as the Titans crafted crude weapons and armor, preparing for what they saw as an inevitable battle - not with the hominids, but with the rest of the lizardkin.

"The small ones think they own us," Nimatowin said, holding a hammer in his claw. "We will show them what true strength is."

Kwekwe's enclave flourished in their isolation, but their separation became increasingly political. Rumors spread of Kwekwe questioning the priests' authority and even discussing the possibility of claiming the pyramid for the Venomous Elite alone.

"They call us poison," Kwekwe said to her followers, "but they depend on us. Without us, they are nothing. It is time they feared us as much as they fear the stars."

V-KAR'S EPIC

The Berserkers' chambers were on the brink of chaos. Akuaq, unshackled during an experimental release, led a group of his kin in a violent outburst that resulted in multiple deaths. The priests argued for culling the Berserkers, but Kaerik objected.

"They are dangerous," Kaerik admitted, "but they are also our last hope. When the Hegemon awakens, they will be his army. Do not let fear blind you to their purpose."

The Council Of Stars

In the central chamber of the pyramid, the lizardkin's ruling council gathered under the carved celestial map of their sacred constellations. Rhazyn, aged and weary, presided over the meeting, flanked by Kaerik and Wigwas.

"The stars are clear," Kaerik began. "The time of the Hegemon's awakening is upon us. Without him, we will fall - either to the hominids or to ourselves."

Rhazyn's tail flicked uneasily. "Waking the Hegemon is not a choice to be made lightly. What if he sees our division as failure? What if he deems us unworthy of his leadership?"

Wigwas, always pragmatic, leaned forward. "If we wait any longer, there may be nothing left for him to awaken to. The Titans are arming themselves, the Venomous Elite are separating, and the Berserkers are on the verge of tearing through the city."

The debate raged late into the night, each voice adding urgency to the decision. Finally, Rhazyn rose to his feet.

"Prepare the rituals," he said. "The Hegemon will awaken."

The Ritual Of Fire

The priests worked tirelessly to prepare the chamber of V-Kar's slumber. Incense filled the air, the scent mingling with the faint musk of the sacred symbols that glowed faintly on the walls. Torches lined the chamber, their flames casting flickering shadows across the ancient carvings.

Kaerik led the chant, his voice resonant and commanding. The lizardkin gathered in silence, their eyes fixed on the sleeping form of their Hegemon.

"V-Kar, Hegemon of fire, leader of the chosen," Kaerik intoned. "Awaken, and guide your people once more. The stars call to you. The earth trembles for you. We beseech you to rise."

The chamber grew still, the air heavy with anticipation.

The Awakening

V-Kar's golden eyes opened.

The room seemed to shudder as he rose, his massive frame uncoiling with deliberate precision. His gaze swept across the chamber, sharp and calculating. The gathered lizardkin knelt, their heads bowed in reverence.

V-Kar's voice, deep and steady, broke the silence. "Why have you woken me?"

V-KAR'S EPIC

Kaerik stepped forward, his claws clasped in respect. "Great Hegemon, your people face their greatest trial. The hominids above grow stronger, and our unity below falters. We need your guidance."

V-Kar's gaze lingered on the high priest, then shifted to Rhazyn. "You were chosen to lead. Have you failed me?"

Rhazyn met the Hegemon's eyes, his voice steady despite his fear. "I have done what I could, but the divisions among us run deep. Only you can unite us, my Hegemon."

Judgment And Resolution

V-Kar turned his attention to the crowd. "You, my people, were chosen for strength, cunning, and purpose. Yet I wake to whispers of rebellion, isolation, and chaos. Explain."

The murmurs that rippled through the crowd were silenced by a single roar from Nimatowin. The Titan stepped forward, his massive frame dwarfing those around him. "We are the strength of this city, yet we are treated like beasts. We deserve more!"

Kwekwe joined him, her voice sharp and defiant. "And we, the Venomous Elite, are seen as outcasts despite our power. Why should we serve those who fear us?"

V-Kar's eyes narrowed. "And the Berserkers? Are they also crying for pity?"

Akuaq, restrained by his handlers, snarled but said nothing.

V-KAR'S EPIC

V-Kar raised a claw, silencing the room. "You forget your purpose. This city exists because of unity. Without it, you are nothing. Strength, poison, rage - these are tools, not masters. I will tolerate no more division."

The New Plan

V-Kar turned to Rhazyn. "You have done well to hold the city together, but your time is over. I will choose a new king."

The crowd tensed as V-Kar moved among them, his golden eyes scanning each face. He stopped before Wigwas, his gaze piercing.

"You have faced the hominids, seen their strength, and survived," he said. "You understand the challenge we face. You will lead."

Wigwas knelt, her head bowed. "I will not fail you, Hegemon."

V-Kar returned to the center of the chamber. "We will not fight the hominids as we are. You will breed strength, discipline, and cunning into your bloodlines. We will strike when the stars align, and we will take back what is ours."

The lizardkin erupted in a roar of renewed purpose. The Titans lowered their weapons, the Venomous Elite stepped back into the fold, and the Berserkers were promised the battles they craved.

A Fragile Unity

V-KAR'S EPIC

As V-Kar retreated to the depths of the cave to resume his slumber, Wigwas took her place as the new king. The city, though still fractured, began the slow process of rebuilding its unity.

But the hominids above continued to thrive, their settlements growing ever larger, their tools more advanced. The lizardkin's path to reclaiming the surface would be long and treacherous.

Deep in his chamber, V-Kar rested, the faint glow of the symbols reflecting in his golden eyes. He had given his people a chance, but he knew that their true test had only just begun.

Chapter 20: Unity At Any Cost

Wigwas's rise to power marked a turning point for the lizardkin. As the newly appointed king, she understood that survival no longer depended on martial prowess alone. The hominids' greatest strength - one that had evaded the lizardkin for centuries - was their sheer numbers. They reproduced quickly, banded together, and adapted relentlessly.

For the lizardkin to stand a chance, Wigwas knew they had to do something they had avoided for far too long: unite the clans.

The Titans, the Venomous Elite, the Berserkers, and the remaining unmarked laborers had to work together, not as divided factions but as a singular force. Wigwas was determined to achieve this unity - no matter the cost.

The Council Of Clans

Wigwas wasted no time. Within days of her coronation, she called for a gathering of representatives from every faction. The Titans, Venomous Elite, Berserkers, priests, scientists, and even the unmarked laborers assembled in the great council chamber beneath the pyramid.

The tension in the air was palpable. The Titans loomed at the edges, their massive frames casting long shadows over the others. The Venomous Elite stood apart, their presence marked by the faint, acrid tang of their toxins. The Berserkers shifted restlessly, their handlers gripping chains that strained under their raw strength.

V-KAR'S EPIC

Wigwas stood at the center, her sharp eyes scanning the room. She raised her claw, commanding silence.

"For too long," she began, her voice steady and commanding, "we have been divided. We have allowed our differences to weaken us while our enemies grow stronger. This ends today."

She turned to Nimatowin, the leader of the Titans. "You say you are the foundation of this city. Prove it. Lend your strength not just to stone and metal, but to our people. Stand with us, and you will no longer be seen as mere tools."

Nimatowin's eyes narrowed, but he nodded slowly. "We will see."

Next, Wigwas addressed Kwekwe of the Venomous Elite. "Your power is unmatched. I offer you the respect you have long deserved. In return, I ask for your loyalty. Together, we will create a force the hominids cannot withstand."

Kwekwe tilted her head, her tongue flicking briefly. "And if we refuse?"

Wigwas stepped closer, her gaze unwavering. "Then you will fall alone, and the stars will forget you."

The Venomous Elite murmured among themselves before Kwekwe finally inclined her head. "We will join you - for now."

Finally, Wigwas turned to the Berserkers. Their leader, Akuaq, snarled, his chains rattling. "We crave battle," he growled. "What will you offer us?"

Wigwas's lips curled into a cold smile. "Battle is coming, Akuaq. But if you wish to fight, you must prove you can be controlled. Follow me, and I will give you more blood than you can dream of. Defy me, and your blood will be the first spilled."

The Berserkers growled but fell silent, their handlers tightening their grip on the chains.

Unity Forged In Fear

The council ended with an uneasy alliance. The factions agreed to work together, though distrust lingered. Wigwas, ever pragmatic, knew this unity was fragile. She did not rely on promises or trust; she relied on fear and necessity.

To cement their cooperation, she implemented new laws:

Mandatory Cross-Training: Titans would train alongside Berserkers to temper their strength with discipline. Venomous Elite would share their knowledge of toxins with the scientists, who in turn would create more effective weapons for all.

Shared Chambers: The factions were forced to live and work together in integrated chambers, breaking down centuries of isolation.

Punishment for Dissent: Any faction caught acting against another would face public execution - a warning to all.

Wigwas ruled with an iron claw, her decisions swift and unyielding. Those who opposed her quickly found themselves removed, their absence a grim reminder of her resolve.

The First Combined Effort

Wigwas's first test of this fragile unity came in the form of a surface raid. The scouts had identified a new hominid settlement near the edge of the forest, its population larger than any the lizardkin had encountered before.

Wigwas assembled a force unlike any the city had seen in centuries: Titans carrying massive, reinforced shields; Venomous Elite armed with poison-coated weapons; Berserkers unleashed at the front lines; and scientists providing guidance on strategy and traps.

The raid was meticulously planned. Wigwas led the force herself, her presence a symbol of the new unity she demanded.

The attack began at dusk, the lizardkin emerging from the shadows like a tidal wave. The hominids, caught off guard, scrambled to defend themselves.

The Titans broke through their primitive walls with ease, their shields deflecting the crude spears and arrows. The Venomous Elite struck quickly and efficiently, their toxins spreading chaos among the defenders. The Berserkers unleashed their fury, tearing through the hominid ranks with terrifying speed.

V-KAR'S EPIC

The battle was brutal and bloody, but by dawn, the settlement lay in ruins. The lizardkin returned to their underground city with supplies, tools, and a newfound sense of strength.

The Price Of Unity

Despite the victory, cracks in the alliance remained. The Venomous Elite complained that they had been used as expendable assassins, while the Berserkers demanded more freedom after their success. The Titans, though satisfied with their role, remained wary of the priests, whom they still viewed as manipulators.

Wigwas addressed these concerns with characteristic pragmatism. She rewarded each faction with privileges suited to their contributions:

The Titans were given new forges and larger quarters.

The Venomous Elite were granted an exclusive chamber for their enclave, though it remained under strict supervision.

The Berserkers were allowed limited, monitored freedom to train and roam within designated areas.

Wigwas knew these concessions would not eliminate the tension, but they would buy her time to solidify her power.

A Growing Threat

As the lizardkin celebrated their victory, the hominids regrouped. Survivors from the ruined settlement spread

Page 107

warnings to nearby villages, their stories of scaled warriors uniting the once-fragmented hominid tribes.

The lizardkin's unity had given them a temporary advantage, but the hominids were proving as adaptable as ever. Their weapons became more sophisticated, their settlements better fortified.

Wigwas knew the raids could not continue indefinitely. The lizardkin needed a new strategy - one that would allow them to reclaim the surface without sparking an endless war.

A New Era

Wigwas stood at the entrance of the great pyramid, gazing up at the stars that had guided her people for generations. The constellations seemed to pulse with quiet wisdom, their patterns unchanging even as the world below shifted.

"Our strength is in our unity," she murmured. "But unity is only the beginning. To truly rise, we must evolve."

With her claws clenched and her resolve unshaken, Wigwas turned back to the city. The path ahead was uncertain, but she knew one thing for sure: the lizardkin would not be defeated - not by the hominids, not by their own divisions, and not by the weight of time itself.

Chapter 21: Dragons Of The Deep

Wigwas sat at the heart of the great council chamber, surrounded by her advisors and representatives from each caste. The stars had spoken, or so the priests claimed, and Wigwas's vision had taken shape: the Berserkers would become dragons, creatures of strength, speed, and freedom unmatched by anything the hominids or even the lizardkin had ever known.

To achieve this, Wigwas needed the cooperation of all factions. The Titans would build enormous caverns to house these future dragons, the Venomous Elite would handle the subtle infiltration of the hominids, and the scientists would oversee the breeding program that would turn vision into reality.

The Berserkers' Rebirth

When Wigwas presented her plan to the Berserkers, she framed it not as a demand but as an opportunity.

"You crave freedom," she said, addressing Akuaq and the others. "You have always been caged, restrained. But as dragons, you will be unstoppable. The skies will be yours to command, the earth beneath you will tremble. This is not control; this is liberation."

Akuaq's eyes gleamed with a mix of rage and wonder. "And you will make this possible?"

Wigwas nodded. "It will take time, but yes. You will be the first of your kind."

The Berserkers, for the first time in centuries, roared in approval. The thought of transformation, of becoming creatures of pure strength and freedom, ignited their fiery spirits.

The Titans' Herculean Task

The construction of the dragon caverns fell to the Titans, whose strength made them the only ones capable of such a monumental task. Wigwas outlined the plan:

Vast Caverns: The Titans would carve enormous chambers into the rock beneath the pyramid, large enough to house fully grown dragons.

Hidden Entrances: The caverns would have no exits to the surface, ensuring the dragons could only leave when the time was right. The entrances would be sealed, ready to be broken through later.

Reinforced Walls: The chambers would be fortified to contain the Berserkers during their transformations, ensuring they could not escape prematurely.

Nimatowin, still skeptical of Wigwas's leadership, confronted her in the council chamber. "You ask much of us," he growled. "Why should we waste our strength on this?"

Wigwas's eyes narrowed. "You are not wasting your strength. You are building a future - a future where the Titans will not just carry stones but stand as the architects of our rise. Refuse, and you will find yourself irrelevant when the dragons rule the skies."

Reluctantly, Nimatowin agreed, and the Titans began their labor.

The Venomous Elite's Mission

While the Berserkers dreamed of soaring through the skies and the Titans toiled deep in the earth, the Venomous Elite were given a far subtler task. Wigwas ordered them to infiltrate small hominid gatherings, not with brute force but with cunning.

Kwekwe led the mission, her venom-coated claws ready to strike. But her orders were clear: "Try to befriend them first. Learn their ways, their weaknesses. If they accept you, exploit it. If they reject you, ensure they do not live to warn others."

The Venomous Elite moved silently through the forest, their presence barely more than a whisper in the night. They targeted isolated hominid settlements, approaching cautiously and observing from the shadows.

One group encountered a small family of hominids gathered around a fire. Kwekwe stepped forward, her movements slow and deliberate. She mimicked the hominids' gestures, extending her claws in what she hoped was a sign of peace.

The hominids hesitated, their expressions wary but curious. They murmured among themselves, their primitive language incomprehensible to Kwekwe.

She crouched low, tilting her head as she observed their reactions. One of the younger hominids approached her, holding out a piece of cooked meat. Kwekwe accepted it, mimicking the act of eating.

But not all encounters ended peacefully. Another Venomous scout, less patient than Kwekwe, attempted the same approach but was met with hostility. When the hominids raised their spears, the scout struck swiftly, her venom-tipped claws slicing through her attackers. She returned to Kwekwe with blood on her scales and no new knowledge gained.

Kwekwe reported her findings to Wigwas. "Some will accept us," she said. "But most will not. Their fear of us runs deep."

"Then we will use that fear," Wigwas replied. "And when the time comes, we will turn it against them."

The Scientists' Breakthrough
The breeding program, led by the city's shunned scientists, was the cornerstone of Wigwas's plan. Drakess, the lead scientist, worked tirelessly in his laboratory, studying the Berserkers' physiology and cross-referencing it with the traits of flying reptiles that still roamed the skies above.

Drakess presented his findings to Wigwas. "The transformation will not be easy," he warned. "The Berserkers' bodies will need to grow larger, their bones lighter but stronger. Wings will require generations of careful breeding, and even then, their instincts may reject the change."

"Do it," Wigwas said without hesitation. "The Berserkers have waited centuries for their freedom. If we must wait a few more generations, so be it. Just ensure it works."

The First Dragons

The first generation of dragon-blooded Berserkers was born within a decade. They were not yet true dragons, but their forms showed the beginning of the transformation. Small, membranous wings sprouted from their backs, their scales grew thicker, and their muscles became more defined.

The Berserkers embraced the changes eagerly, their desire for freedom outweighing any discomfort. Akuaq, now viewed as the father of the dragon-bloodline, watched over the younglings with pride.

"They will fly," he said, his voice filled with conviction. "And when they do, the world will tremble."

A City Transformed

As the years passed, the underground city became a hive of activity. The dragon caverns expanded, the breeding program continued, and the Venomous Elite perfected their infiltration techniques.

But Wigwas knew the path ahead was still treacherous. The hominids grew more organized with each passing year, their settlements larger and their weapons deadlier.

V-KAR'S EPIC

The lizardkin had set their plan into motion, but the true test would come when the dragons emerged from the depths.

Wigwas stood at the entrance of the pyramid, gazing up at the stars. "They will never see us coming," she murmured. "And when they do, it will be too late."

Chapter 22: The Dragons Take Shape

Deep within the underground city, the first generation of dragon-blooded Berserkers grew into their monstrous forms. The transformation was not yet complete, but the changes were undeniable. Their wings, once fragile and stunted, now spanned several feet, their membranes thickening with each molt. Their claws lengthened, their muscles rippled with power, and their fiery tempers seemed to burn brighter than ever.

Akuaq, the leader of the Berserkers, stood at the forefront of this evolution. His own wings were larger than those of the others, and his roar, deep and resonant, echoed through the caverns like the rumble of distant thunder. The younger Berserkers idolized him, mimicking his movements and hanging on his every word.

But the transformation came with its challenges.

The Pain Of Evolution

The process of becoming dragon-blooded was not without its price. Many of the Berserkers suffered from growing pains, their wings aching as the bones and muscles stretched to accommodate flight. Others experienced imbalance as their changing forms disrupted their center of gravity, causing clumsiness that frustrated their naturally aggressive instincts.

"You call this freedom?" one young Berserker snarled after stumbling during a training session. "We're weak. We're broken."

V-KAR'S EPIC

Akuaq silenced him with a single swipe of his claw.
"Weakness is temporary," he growled. "Freedom is worth
any pain. If you cannot endure, you do not deserve to fly."

The words resonated with the Berserkers, reigniting their
fiery determination. They pushed through the pain, training
tirelessly in the vast caverns carved by the Titans. Their
strength grew, their wings flapped harder, and their bodies
began to resemble the dragons Wigwas envisioned.

The Venomous Elite's Silent War
While the Berserkers adapted to their new forms, the
Venomous Elite continued their mission on the surface.
Kwekwe led her agents with precision, targeting small
hominid gatherings in a campaign of subtle infiltration and
silent assassination.

Their orders were clear: gain the trust of the hominids if
possible, and eliminate them if not.

Kwekwe herself excelled at blending in, her movements
fluid and deliberate. She approached a group of hominids
near the edge of a forest one night, her claws sheathed and
her posture low. The hominids hesitated, their primitive
language forming guttural whispers as they debated her
intentions.

She extended her claws slowly, placing them on the ground
as a gesture of peace. A younger hominid, barely more
than a child, stepped forward, offering her a crude bowl of
water. Kwekwe mimicked gratitude, taking the bowl and
sipping carefully.

The encounter seemed successful - until one of the older hominids spotted the faint sheen of venom dripping from her claw.

"They're not to be trusted!" the elder shouted, raising his spear.

Before Kwekwe could react, chaos erupted. Her agents emerged from the shadows, striking with swift, venomous precision. The hominids fell quickly, their cries silenced before they could reach the nearby settlement.

Kwekwe stood over the bodies, her expression unreadable. "They could not understand us," she said to her team. "So they will not survive us."

Successes And Failures

The Venomous Elite's missions were a mix of triumph and frustration. Some hominid groups were receptive to their overtures of peace, offering food and shelter in exchange for perceived goodwill. These interactions provided valuable insight into the hominids' behavior, their weaknesses, and their strengths.

But more often than not, the missions ended in bloodshed. The hominids' fear of the unknown ran deep, and even the slightest misstep could turn cautious acceptance into violent rejection.

Kwekwe reported her findings to Wigwas. "They are clever," she said. "They sense danger even when we mask it. Gaining their trust is possible, but maintaining it is precarious. One mistake, one drop of venom too visible, and it all collapses."

Wigwas nodded, her expression thoughtful. "Your work is not for nothing. Fear and trust are two sides of the same blade. We will wield both when the time comes."

Collaboration In The Shadows

For the first time in generations, the Berserkers and Venomous Elite began to collaborate. Wigwas, ever pragmatic, saw the value in uniting their strengths. The Venomous Elite taught the young dragon-blooded Berserkers how to fight with precision, tempering their raw aggression with calculated strikes.

In turn, the Berserkers shared their boundless energy and determination, inspiring the Venomous Elite to push beyond their limits. The bond between the two factions, though tenuous, began to grow.

Akuaq and Kwekwe, once distrustful of one another, began to find common ground.

"We are the future of our people," Akuaq said during a rare moment of calm. "Strength and venom, fire and shadow. Together, we will be unstoppable."

Kwekwe tilted her head, her tongue flicking thoughtfully. "For now," she replied. "But do not mistake cooperation for unity. We walk the same path, but our destinations may differ."

Akuaq grinned, his sharp teeth glinting. "As long as the path leads to blood and freedom, I care little where it ends."

Preparing For The Sky

As the Berserkers continued to grow into their dragon-blooded forms, the Titans completed their work on the caverns. The chambers were vast, their walls reinforced to withstand the strength and fury of the growing dragons.

The final stage of the plan required an escape route to the surface. The Titans, under Wigwas's orders, began digging a massive tunnel that would allow the dragons to emerge when the time was right.

Wigwas herself oversaw the progress, her sharp gaze ensuring that every detail was accounted for. She knew the risk of revealing their plans too early, but the reward was worth it.

"When the dragons rise," she said to her council, "the hominids will not know what hit them. Their fire will rain down, and the sky will belong to us."

A Fragile Alliance

Despite their progress, the alliance between the Berserkers and Venomous Elite remained fragile. Akuaq's desire for freedom clashed with Kwekwe's preference for subtlety, and their differing philosophies often led to tension.

V-KAR'S EPIC

"We should strike now," Akuaq argued during a council meeting. "The hominids grow stronger every day. Give us the chance, and we will tear them apart."

Kwekwe shook her head. "And lose everything in the process? The hominids may fear you, but they are clever. They will adapt. Rushing in blindly will only lead to failure."

Wigwas silenced them both with a raised claw. "Patience," she said. "The dragons are not yet ready, and neither are the hominids. When the time comes, we will strike as one. Until then, you will do as I command."

A Glimpse Of The Future

As Wigwas watched the young dragons spread their wings in the vast caverns, she allowed herself a moment of satisfaction. The lizardkin's strength was growing, their unity - though fragile - was holding, and their enemies above remained blissfully unaware of the storm that brewed below.

"The sky will burn," she murmured to herself. "And when it does, we will rise."

Chapter 23: The Venomous Creed

Kwekwe stood in the shadow of a massive tree on the forest's edge, her golden eyes fixed on the distant glow of a hominid settlement. Behind her, the Venomous Elite moved silently, their scales blending with the underbrush. Tonight, their mission was not one of death, but of deception.

For months, Kwekwe and her agents had been observing the hominids, studying their primitive beliefs and rituals. The hominids' fear of the unknown made them susceptible to manipulation, and Kwekwe saw an opportunity to seed chaos from within.

"Their minds are weak," she told her followers. "They worship what they cannot understand. We will give them gods to follow - gods that serve us."

The Rise Of The Serpent Gods

The Venomous Elite began their work carefully, infiltrating small hominid gatherings and planting the seeds of a new religion. Using their natural charisma and the hominids' fascination with serpents, they spun tales of serpent gods - mighty deities who ruled the heavens and the earth.

Kwekwe herself took on the role of a divine messenger, appearing to hominid tribes cloaked in a ceremonial robe made of woven leaves and feathers. Her movements were slow and deliberate, her voice soft yet commanding.

V-KAR'S EPIC

"You are lost," she told them, her words carefully chosen. "But the Serpent Gods have seen your struggle. They offer you guidance, if you will only listen."

The hominids, awed by her presence and the sheer otherworldliness of her appearance, began to accept her words.

<u>Symbols Of Faith</u>

The Venomous Elite used their knowledge of the lizardkin's ancient symbols to create new ones for the hominids to worship. These symbols, carved into stone or painted on wood, depicted coiling serpents with wings of fire and venom dripping from their fangs.

The symbols became central to the rituals the Venomous Elite introduced. Fires were lit, offerings of food and carved trinkets were made, and chants were taught - chants that subtly reinforced obedience to the "messengers" of the serpent gods.

Kwekwe's agents fanned out, spreading these symbols and rituals to nearby hominid settlements. Each new group they encountered was told the same story:

"The Serpent Gods bring strength. They will protect you from your enemies. Honor them, and they will lead you to glory."

<u>Followers Of The Serpent</u>

The hominids who accepted the serpent gods began forming small, devoted cults. These groups grew rapidly, their members drawn together by shared fear and hope.

One cult leader, a young hominid named Rath, became particularly fervent in his belief. Rath claimed to have received visions from the serpent gods, and he led his followers with zealous determination.

Kwekwe observed Rath closely, ensuring his loyalty remained with her and her agents. When doubts arose among his followers, she would appear, cloaked in her ceremonial garb, to reaffirm his position.

"The gods have chosen you," she whispered to Rath during one such visit. "Lead them well, and you will be rewarded."

Challenges And Resistance

Not all hominids were so easily swayed. In some settlements, the appearance of the Venomous Elite was met with suspicion and hostility. One group of hominid warriors ambushed a Venomous agent, wounding him before he could escape.

Word spread of "false gods" among the more skeptical hominid tribes, and resistance began to form. These groups warned others to reject the serpent cults, labeling them as dangerous and corrupt.

Kwekwe, ever calculating, responded with both diplomacy and force.

To the skeptical tribes, she sent emissaries to offer peace and demonstrate the supposed benevolence of the serpent gods. If they refused, the Venomous Elite struck swiftly and silently, eliminating key leaders and leaving behind symbols of the serpent gods as warnings.

"Let them see the power of what they deny," Kwekwe told her agents. "Their fear will turn to faith - or silence."

The Spread Of Chaos

As the serpent cults grew, so did the divisions among the hominids. Tribes that embraced the serpent gods clashed with those that rejected them, their conflicts escalating into skirmishes and raids.

Kwekwe watched from the shadows, pleased with the results. The hominids, once united in their growing strength, were now fractured. Their focus shifted inward, their energy spent on fighting one another rather than expanding their settlements or developing new tools.

But Kwekwe knew this was only the beginning.

A Meeting With Wigwas

Kwekwe returned to the underground city to report her progress to Wigwas. The council chamber was dimly lit, the faint glow of the sacred symbols reflecting off the walls.

"The serpent cults are spreading," Kwekwe said, her tone measured. "The hominids are divided. Their strength diminishes with each passing day."

Wigwas nodded, her expression thoughtful. "And their resistance?"

"It exists," Kwekwe admitted. "But it is disorganized. Those who oppose us lack the numbers or cohesion to pose a serious threat."

Wigwas's lips curled into a faint smile. "Good. Let their gods divide them further. When the dragons rise, they will face a sky filled with fire and a ground filled with chaos. They will not stand a chance."

The Serpent's Hold

The serpent cults continued to grow, their influence spreading like a slow, insidious poison. Some hominids began building primitive temples in honor of the serpent gods, their crude structures adorned with the symbols crafted by the Venomous Elite.

Rath's following became one of the largest and most devoted, his influence extending to several nearby tribes. He led rituals with fervor, his voice ringing out in praise of the gods he believed were guiding him.

Kwekwe watched him closely, her mind already turning to the next phase of the plan.

"We have sown the seeds," she said to her agents. "Now we must let them grow. When the time comes, the serpent gods will strike - and the hominids will fall."

Chapter 24: The Scattering Of The Venomous Elite

The Venomous Elite, once united in their silent and deadly purpose, began to fracture under the weight of their success. As their serpent cults spread across the hominid tribes, disagreements arose among Kwekwe's agents. Some believed they should remain true to their mission of manipulation and chaos, while others argued for a more direct role in shaping the surface world.

"We've done enough," hissed Kaelyss, a younger Venomous agent. "The hominids fight among themselves. Let them destroy each other while we return to the depths."

Kwekwe's response was sharp and cutting. "And leave them unchecked? Foolish. Their strength lies in their ability to adapt. If we leave them to their own devices, they will rise again."

But Kaelyss was not alone in her doubts. Rumors of dissent spread through the Venomous ranks, and quiet tensions grew into open disputes.

The Breaking Point

The fracture came during a mission to expand the influence of the serpent cults. A small group of Venomous agents, led by Kwekwe, infiltrated a new hominid settlement, but disagreements over tactics turned into a heated argument.

"This is not our way!" shouted Draykarn, an elder Venomous. "We are assassins, not caretakers. We were bred for death, not this… play at gods!"

Kwekwe's claws flexed, her venom dripping to the ground. "We are whatever our people need us to be. If you cannot see that, then leave. But know this: without our guidance, the hominids will become a greater threat than you can imagine."

Draykarn snarled but did not strike. Instead, he and a handful of his followers turned their backs on Kwekwe and disappeared into the forest.

V-KAR'S EPIC

Scattered Across The Surface

As the tensions boiled over, more Venomous agents began to abandon their mission, scattering across the surface. Some sought solitude in the wilderness, while others found refuge among the very hominids they once sought to manipulate.

These scattered Venomous, no longer bound by Kwekwe's authority, began to teach the hominids rudimentary skills. Their growls and hisses became the basis of crude languages, blending with the guttural sounds already used by the hominids. Over time, this shared communication evolved into structured tongues, allowing the hominids to organize more effectively.

Teaching Civilization

The Venomous who remained with the hominids began to influence their development in subtle but profound ways.

Shelter: Drawing on their knowledge of underground construction, the Venomous taught the hominids how to build sturdier structures. Mud and wood huts gave way to stone buildings, and eventually, small walled villages.

Tools: Using their understanding of metallurgy from the lizardkin city, they introduced the hominids to basic smelting and forging techniques, enabling them to craft better weapons and tools.

Language: The hybrid tongue of growls and hisses spread quickly, uniting disparate hominid tribes under a common means of communication.

These contributions laid the foundation for the first hominid cities, small but growing centers of trade and governance.

Castles In The Hills

As the hominids advanced, they began constructing larger, more fortified structures. Inspired by the natural strength of caves and mountains, they built castles into the hills, their thick stone walls designed to protect against both natural predators and rival tribes.

The Venomous, watching from the shadows, marveled at how quickly the hominids adapted. What had started as crude villages were now becoming strongholds, their banners flying proudly in the wind.

But the Venomous also ensured that fear lingered in the hearts of their new allies.

The Legend Of The Serpent Lords

The scattered Venomous spread rumors of great flying serpents - creatures of fire and shadow that ruled the underworld. They whispered tales of dragons that slumbered beneath the earth, ready to rise and rain destruction on any who dared venture too deeply into caves.

These stories took root in the minds of the hominids, passed down through generations. Parents told their children to avoid dark places, to never explore the depths of the earth for fear of awakening the wrath of the serpent lords.

The rumors served their purpose: the hominids became cautious of caves and tunnels, their curiosity tempered by fear.

Kwekwe's Reflection

From her perch in a dense forest, Kwekwe watched the rise of the hominid cities with mixed emotions. Her agents were scattered, her authority diminished, but her influence lingered in the very foundations of hominid civilization.

"They are clever," she murmured to herself, her claws tracing the serpent symbol she had once carved into a stone tablet. "Too clever. But their fear will keep them in check… for now."

She knew the hominids would continue to grow, their ingenuity unmatched. But she also knew the lizardkin, hidden in their underground city, were preparing for the day when the dragons would rise and reclaim the surface.

A New Balance

As the centuries passed, the lizardkin remained hidden, their strength growing in secret. The hominids, guided in part by the Venomous, built kingdoms above. The legends of the serpent gods and flying dragons persisted, shaping their fears and beliefs.

The stage was set for a future clash - one where the lizardkin would emerge from the depths, their fire and fury challenging the very civilizations they had helped create.

V-KAR'S EPIC

Chapter 25: The Myth Of The Serpent Gods

The whispers of the serpent gods had taken on a life of their own among the hominids. What began as scattered cults grew into sprawling myths that shaped the very core of their developing civilizations. Each village and kingdom adapted the stories to their own culture, adding layers of meaning and significance.

At the heart of these myths was the belief in the serpent gods - powerful, otherworldly beings who ruled with both fearsome wrath and boundless wisdom. Most hominids revered them as deities to be feared and appeased. But as the stories spread and evolved, a new interpretation emerged.

The Misguided Prophet

Among the hominids was a young, charismatic leader named Erian, who claimed to have received a vision from the serpent gods themselves. Unlike the traditional tales of wrath and destruction, Erian's vision spoke of the serpent gods as loving, all-knowing, and endlessly compassionate.

"The serpents do not seek to harm us," Erian proclaimed to a gathering of villagers. "They are not creatures of fire and venom, but beings of light and understanding. They guide us not through fear, but through love."

His words struck a chord with the downtrodden and desperate, those who longed for a source of hope in a harsh and unpredictable world. Erian's perspective spread quickly, his followers growing in number with each passing week.

Page 133

V-KAR'S EPIC

The Flood Of Belief

Erian's teachings became a unifying force among the hominids. Tribes that once warred over resources and territory now came together under his banner, inspired by his vision of a benevolent serpent pantheon.

Temples were built in honor of the loving serpent gods, their walls adorned with intricate carvings of serpents coiled around stars and moons. Priests and priestesses recited Erian's teachings, their voices rising in chants that echoed through the valleys.

"The serpents are our protectors," they preached. "They will guide us to a world without fear, without pain."

The movement became a flood, sweeping across the land. Kingdoms that once stood divided found themselves united under this shared belief, their banners flying the symbol of the serpent entwined with the sun.

A Dangerous Misinterpretation

But not everyone accepted Erian's vision. Among the hominids were skeptics and traditionalists who clung to the older, darker myths of the serpent gods. They viewed Erian's teachings as blasphemy, a dangerous distortion of the truth.

"The serpents are not kind," warned Hestan, a grizzled elder from a distant tribe. "They are creatures of the underworld, born of fire and shadow. To trust them is to invite ruin."

V-KAR'S EPIC

Hestan's warnings went largely unheeded, but his words planted seeds of doubt in the minds of some. These doubters formed secret groups, determined to uncover the true nature of the serpent gods.

V-Kar Awakens

While the hominids' beliefs grew and evolved, the lizardkin below stirred with anticipation. Deep in the heart of their underground city, the ancient chamber of V-Kar glowed faintly as the symbols on its walls pulsed with energy.

The lizardkin gathered in silence as their Hegemon slowly rose from his long slumber. His massive frame, coiled with muscle and scales that gleamed like polished stone, filled the chamber. His golden eyes opened, piercing and unyielding.

The priests knelt before him, their voices trembling as they recited the ancient incantations of awakening.

"V-Kar, Great Hegemon, ruler of fire and sky, your people call to you. The time has come to rise once more."

V-Kar stepped forward, his movements deliberate and powerful. His gaze swept across the assembled lizardkin, and when he spoke, his voice was deep and resonant.

"Why have I been woken?"

A Nation United

Wigwas stepped forward, her head bowed in respect. "Great Hegemon, the surface world thrives with our

Page 135

enemies. The hominids have grown strong, their numbers vast. But your people have prepared for this moment. The dragons are ready, and your nation awaits your command."

V-Kar considered her words, his expression unreadable. He turned to the gathered crowd, his voice rising like thunder.

"For centuries, you have waited. For centuries, you have prepared. The time for waiting is over."

The lizardkin erupted in a roar of approval, their voices echoing through the vast underground chambers. The Titans stood tall, their massive frames radiating strength. The Venomous Elite, scattered but loyal, returned to the fold, their venomous claws gleaming. The dragon-blooded Berserkers spread their wings, their fiery tempers barely contained.

Preparing The Dragons

Under V-Kar's leadership, the lizardkin focused all their efforts on preparing the dragons for their ascension. The Titans began digging the final tunnels to the surface, creating massive exits that would allow the dragons to soar freely when the time came.

The Venomous Elite, now fully united under Kwekwe's command, infiltrated the hominids' growing cities, spreading rumors and further stoking the fear of serpents from the underworld. These whispers only reinforced the hominids' myths, ensuring they would not venture too deeply into the caves.

Meanwhile, the Berserkers trained relentlessly, their wings beating against the air as they practiced flight in the vast caverns. Akuaq, their leader, roared in triumph as he soared through the underground skies, his shadow stretching across the cavern walls.

"The sky will belong to us!" Akuaq bellowed, his voice filled with fury and pride. "The world will tremble when the dragons rise!"

A New Purpose

As the preparations continued, V-Kar gathered his council to discuss their final plans. Wigwas, Kwekwe, Akuaq, and Nimatowin stood before him, each representing a vital part of the lizardkin's strength.

"The hominids are united under false gods," Wigwas said. "Their belief in the serpent's love blinds them to our true nature."

"Then we will show them the truth," V-Kar replied. "The dragons will rise, and the surface will burn. They will learn what it means to fear us."

The council nodded, their resolve unshaken.

The Calm Before The Storm

As the lizardkin prepared for their ascent, the surface world remained blissfully unaware of the storm that brewed below. The hominids continued to build their temples and chant their prayers, their faith in the serpent gods unshaken.

V-KAR'S EPIC

But the whispers of doubt and fear lingered, carried on the wind like a distant echo.

And deep beneath the earth, the dragons waited, their wings stretching, their claws sharpening, their fury building.

The time of reckoning was near.

Chapter 26: The Dragons Emerge

The earth trembled. Deep below the surface, within the great pyramid that had stood for millennia, the lizardkin's preparations were complete. The massive tunnels carved by the Titans now stretched to the surface, their exits concealed beneath dense forests and jagged cliffs.

In the vast underground chamber where the dragon-blooded Berserkers trained, V-Kar stood at the center, his golden eyes surveying his creations. The dragons, fierce and towering, spread their wings, their fiery breaths lighting the cavern walls. Akuaq, their leader, hovered near the ceiling, his massive wings casting a shadow over the assembled lizardkin.

V-Kar raised a claw, his voice a roar that reverberated through the city. "Today, we reclaim the surface. Today, the dragons rise!"

The Sky Ablaze

The dragons surged upward through the tunnels, their roars shaking the earth as they broke through the concealed exits. Fire and fury erupted from the forests and hills as the first dragons soared into the open sky.

The hominids' settlements were ill-prepared for such an assault. Castles and fortified villages that had taken generations to build were reduced to rubble in hours. The dragons unleashed streams of fire that melted stone and scorched the earth. Their claws tore through walls, their wings flattened towers, and their roars shattered the morale of anyone who dared to resist.

V-KAR'S EPIC

From the ground, the hominids could only watch in horror as the sky turned red with flames and ash. The legends of the flying serpents had become reality, and their wrath was far greater than anyone had imagined.

The Venomous Elite's Escape

Amid the chaos, the Venomous Elite carried out their carefully orchestrated plan. Kwekwe and her agents, who had embedded themselves within the hominids' cities, moved swiftly to secure their positions.

In the largest hominid capital, where Erian's followers had built temples to honor the serpent gods, the Venomous Elite dug deep beneath the city, creating hidden tunnels and chambers. These underground sanctuaries were designed to mirror the great pyramid of V-Kar, a place where the Venomous Elite could hibernate and bide their time.

Kwekwe ensured that her followers remained untouched by the dragons' fury. She marked the castles and settlements that were loyal to her with the symbols of the serpent gods, a sign for the dragons to spare them.

The hominids who resisted or questioned the serpent cults were not as fortunate. Their cities burned, their people scattered, and their faith in the serpent gods shattered in the face of overwhelming destruction.

Slave Convoys To The Pyramid

As the dragons laid waste to the surface, the Venomous Elite began organizing convoys of captured hominids.

These slaves were sent to the great pyramid of V-Kar, where they were forced to labor in the deep mines beneath the structure.

The mines, already vast, were expanded further under the direction of the Titans. Rich veins of ore and precious metals were uncovered, fueling the lizardkin's growing power. The hominid slaves, broken and subdued, worked tirelessly under the watchful eyes of their reptilian overseers.

For the lizardkin, the slaves were not just laborers - they were a reminder of their dominance. The sight of the once-proud hominids now reduced to tools of their oppressors filled the lizardkin with a renewed sense of purpose.

The Dragons' Fury

Akuaq and his dragon-blooded kin reveled in their newfound freedom. They soared over the ruins of the hominid kingdoms, their roars echoing through the valleys. The destruction they wrought was absolute, leaving no castle, village, or temple untouched unless marked by the Venomous Elite.

But the dragons' emergence was not without cost. The sheer force of their attack disrupted the delicate balance the lizardkin had maintained for centuries. The hominids who survived fled into the wilderness, scattering across the land and vowing vengeance.

V-KAR'S EPIC

V-Kar's Command

As the dragons returned to the great pyramid, their wings heavy with exhaustion and their claws still dripping with the remnants of their conquest, V-Kar addressed his people.

"You have done well," he said, his voice filled with cold satisfaction. "The surface is ours, and the hominids have been reminded of their place. But our work is not yet done. The mines must be expanded, the dragons must grow stronger, and the serpent gods must be feared by all."

He turned to Wigwas, who stood at his side. "Ensure the dragons are ready for the next phase. The surface is but the beginning."

The Aftermath

The surface world, once dominated by the hominids, was now a smoldering wasteland of ruins and ash. The castles that had once stood as symbols of their power lay in rubble, their stone walls blackened by dragonfire.

But beneath the earth, the lizardkin thrived. The Venomous Elite retreated to their hidden sanctuaries, their influence over the remaining hominids growing quietly. The Titans and unmarked laborers expanded the mines, digging ever deeper into the earth. The dragons, now the undisputed rulers of the skies, rested and prepared for their next campaign.

And in the heart of it all, V-Kar watched, his golden eyes gleaming with the promise of total domination.

Chapter 27: The Titans Unleashed

In the heart of the great pyramid, V-Kar stood before his council, the towering shadows of the Titans looming behind him. The chamber was filled with an air of reverence and anticipation. The dragons had decimated the surface, the mines were filling with treasures unearthed by captured hominid slaves, and the Venomous Elite had entrenched themselves in hidden strongholds beneath the largest cities of the remaining hominids.

It was time for the next phase of conquest.

V-Kar's Final Command

With his golden eyes gleaming in the dim light of the chamber, V-Kar addressed his people. His voice, deep and commanding, carried the weight of centuries of leadership.

"The dragons have risen," he began, his gaze sweeping across the assembled lizardkin. "The surface trembles beneath our might, and the hominids know true fear. But our work is not done."

He turned to Nimatowin, the leader of the Titans, his massive frame radiating raw power. "You and your kin have labored in the shadows, carving our city and our sanctuaries. Now, you will take what is yours. The earth above belongs to the Titans. Go forth and plunder. Take the forests, the mountains, the rivers - leave nothing unclaimed."

The Titans roared in approval, their voices shaking the very walls of the chamber.

V-KAR'S EPIC

A Solemn Edict

V-Kar raised a claw, silencing the crowd. His tone shifted, colder, more deliberate.

"Let it be known," he said, "that the strongholds of the Venomous Elite are sacred. No Titan, dragon, or warrior is to lay claw upon them. Their work is vital to our cause, and their protection is absolute."

Kwekwe, standing among the council, inclined her head in acknowledgment. "The serpent gods have blessed your wisdom, Hegemon," she said, her voice smooth and calculated.

V-Kar's gaze lingered on her for a moment before returning to the Titans. "You are forbidden from attacking their strongholds. But the rest of the earth is yours to plunder. Take it, and leave no doubt as to who rules this world."

The Titans Emerge

Under Nimatowin's leadership, the Titans stormed to the surface. Their massive frames moved with surprising speed and purpose, their strength unparalleled by anything the hominids had ever encountered. They tore through forests, toppled cliffs, and dammed rivers, reshaping the landscape to suit their needs.

Hominid villages hidden deep in the wilderness were no match for the Titans' raw power. Walls crumbled beneath their fists, and entire settlements were reduced to rubble in hours. Survivors fled in terror, their screams echoing through the valleys.

V-KAR'S EPIC

The Titans were relentless, their plundering a wave of destruction that left nothing untouched.

The Venomous Strongholds

True to V-Kar's command, the Titans avoided the strongholds of the Venomous Elite. These hidden sanctuaries, buried deep beneath the ruins of the largest hominid cities, became centers of power and influence.

Kwekwe and her agents continued their work, spreading the myths of the serpent gods to the remaining hominids. They whispered tales of divine wrath and divine mercy, ensuring that the fear of the lizardkin remained etched into the hearts of their enemies.

Beneath the surface, the Venomous Elite expanded their tunnels, creating intricate networks that connected their sanctuaries to the great pyramid. Slave convoys passed through these hidden passages, delivering resources and treasures to the lizardkin's growing empire.

A Nation Reforged

As the Titans ravaged the land and the Venomous Elite entrenched themselves, the lizardkin nation grew stronger. The dragons rested in their vast caverns, their strength replenished, while the unmarked laborers expanded the mines beneath the pyramid.

V-Kar, satisfied with the progress of his people, returned to his hibernation chamber. Before closing his eyes, he issued one final order to Wigwas and the council.

"Do not wake me until the world is ours," he said. "The surface belongs to the Titans, the skies to the dragons, and the shadows to the Venomous. Leave no stone unturned, no enemy unbroken. Only then will I rise again."

The Titans' Reign

The Titans continued their rampage across the earth, their might unmatched by the scattered and disorganized hominids. They established massive fortresses in the mountains and plains, their towering structures visible for miles.

These fortresses became centers of power, where the Titans stored their spoils and trained their young. They ruled with an iron claw, their dominance a reminder of the lizardkin's supremacy.

The Balance Of Power

The Venomous Elite, despite their isolation, maintained a delicate balance of power with the Titans and dragons. Kwekwe ensured that her agents remained valuable, their influence over the hominids critical to the lizardkin's continued success.

But beneath the surface, tensions simmered. The Titans' growing arrogance, the dragons' fiery tempers, and the Venomous Elite's secrecy threatened to disrupt the fragile unity that V-Kar had built.

For now, the lizardkin remained united, their dominance unchallenged. But the seeds of future conflict were already taking root.

Chapter 28: The Hominids Regroup

The surface world lay in ruin. Once-mighty castles and bustling settlements were reduced to ash and rubble, their inhabitants scattered to the wilderness. The dragons of the lizardkin had unleashed devastation unparalleled in history, yet their reign over the skies was destined to be short-lived.

Flight, though powerful, demanded immense energy. The dragons - fueled by fury, fire, and their unrelenting appetites - soon found themselves struggling to maintain their dominance. The forests were stripped of game, and the hominids, now hiding in smaller, mobile groups, became harder to find. Starvation began to weaken the great dragons, forcing them to abandon the skies.

The Dragons' Retreat

Akuaq, leader of the dragon-blooded Berserkers, stood atop a rocky outcrop overlooking a barren valley. His once-proud wings, scorched and battered from countless battles, hung limply at his sides. Behind him, the remaining dragons gathered, their breaths shallow, their bodies gaunt.

"We cannot fly much longer," growled Kaarn, one of Akuaq's most trusted lieutenants. "There is no food. The skies are empty."

Akuaq's eyes burned with anger, but deep down, he knew Kaarn spoke the truth. The power that had once made them gods of the air was now their greatest weakness.

"We will find a place to rest," Akuaq said finally, his voice heavy. "Somewhere cold, where we can sleep until the earth is ready to bow to us again."

The dragons began their retreat, heading north toward the frozen mountains, where their massive bodies would hibernate in icy caverns. The skies, once filled with their fiery presence, fell silent.

The Titans' Dominance

While the dragons retreated, the Titans continued their reign of terror. Nimatowin and his kin roamed the countryside, their massive forms leaving paths of destruction wherever they went. Villages hidden deep in forests were crushed beneath their feet, and mountain strongholds were torn apart with their bare claws.

But their victories came at a cost. Without the dragons to command the skies, the Titans faced increasing resistance. The hominids, now united in their desperation, began to fight back.

The Hominids Regroup

In the shadows of the ruined castles and scorched forests, the surviving hominids banded together. Their leaders, driven by necessity, forged alliances between once-warring tribes and kingdoms.

"We cannot defeat them through strength alone," said Erian, the misguided prophet whose vision of the serpent gods had inspired hope among the hominids. "But their strength will fade, just as the dragons have fled. We must endure."

The hominids adopted new strategies, using their intelligence and resourcefulness to outmaneuver the Titans. They abandoned static settlements, opting for mobile camps that could disappear at the first sign of danger. They set traps in narrow passes, luring Titans into ambushes where they could be overwhelmed with fire and collapsing terrain.

Slowly but surely, the tide began to turn.

The Power Of Adaptation

One of the most significant developments among the hominids was the rise of advanced tactics and tools. The crude weapons of the past gave way to finely crafted spears, bows, and traps. Blacksmiths, hidden in remote forges, worked tirelessly to create weapons capable of piercing even the Titans' thick hides.

Erian's teachings, though rooted in misguided faith, became a rallying cry for the hominids. He preached resilience and unity, urging his people to see the serpent gods as symbols of strength and survival rather than fear.

"The serpents have left the skies," he told his followers. "But their spirit remains in us. We are their heirs, and we will rise."

V-KAR'S EPIC

The Frozen Dragons

Far to the north, the dragons reached the icy mountains. The cold air bit at their scales, but it also slowed their burning hunger, easing the pain of starvation.

Akuaq led his kin into the frozen caves, their massive forms carving out chambers in the ice. As they settled into their new sanctuaries, their breaths grew slower, their bodies stilling as hibernation claimed them.

"We will sleep," Akuaq growled, his voice echoing through the cavern. "But we will not forget. When the time comes, we will rise again, and the earth will burn."

The dragons' retreat marked the end of their dominance, but their presence lingered in the minds of the hominids, fueling legends that would shape their cultures for generations.

The Titans' Struggle

As the dragons faded into the mountains, the Titans found themselves increasingly isolated. The hominids, though still vulnerable, were becoming more organized and bold. Ambushes became more frequent, and the Titans began to suffer losses for the first time.

Nimatowin, ever defiant, refused to retreat. "We are the lords of this world!" he roared. "No prey can stand against us!"

But even Nimatowin could not deny the growing difficulty of their campaign. The Titans' raw strength was unmatched, but their lack of subtlety left them vulnerable to the hominids' cunning.

The Lizardfolk Below

Beneath the surface, the lizardkin nation remained strong. The mines beneath V-Kar's pyramid continued to produce resources, and the Venomous Elite, now entrenched in their hidden sanctuaries, maintained their influence over the scattered hominids.

Wigwas, now the ruler of the underground city, watched the events above with calculated patience. "Let the Titans plunder," she said to her council. "Let the dragons sleep. The surface will weaken itself, and when the time is right, we will strike again."

A Fragile Peace

For the hominids, the retreat of the dragons and the slow decline of the Titans marked the beginning of a fragile peace. They rebuilt their settlements, cautious of the ever-present threat from the lizardkin below.

The stories of the flying serpents and the towering Titans became myths and warnings, passed down from generation to generation. The caves, still feared as entrances to the underworld, remained untouched, their dark depths hiding the secrets of the lizardkin's empire.

But beneath the earth, V-Kar slumbered, his dreams filled with fire and conquest. The world above belonged to the hominids for now, but the lizardkin knew that their time would come again.

Chapter 29: Rebuilding Supremacy

The lizardkin's dominance, though fractured, persisted. Beneath the surface and in the ruins of the great civilizations they had decimated, the Venomous Elite worked tirelessly to rebuild and consolidate their power. Their remaining strongholds - Atlantis, Babylon, and Mu - stood as shining beacons of their supremacy, each a testament to their cunning and control.

Yet even with their grip on these strongholds, the lizardkin faced new challenges. The hominids, united by their belief in an omni-compassionate god - one they seemed to identify with the sun - were slowly regrouping. Though the lizardkin dismissed the Human faith as folly, they could not ignore its unifying power.

The Stronghold Of Atlantis

Atlantis, a gleaming city built on an island plateau, served as the crown jewel of the lizardkin's surface empire. Here, the Venomous Elite held sway, their influence bolstered by an intricate network of tunnels and chambers carved deep into the earth.

The city's towering walls and shining spires were deceptive; beneath its splendor lay a grim reality. Human captives labored endlessly in the mines and fields, their bodies bent and broken under the weight of their servitude. Yet, curiously, many of these Humans clung to their faith in the loving serpent god.

Kwekwe, now the ruler of Atlantis, viewed this devotion with a mix of curiosity and disdain. "How can they worship us?" she mused aloud during a council meeting. "They suffer beneath our claws, yet they sing praises to a god of compassion. Do they not see the irony?"

Wigwas, attending the meeting from below via a network of tunnels connecting Atlantis to the great pyramid, responded pragmatically. "Faith is a tool, Kwekwe. Let them have their illusions. It keeps them docile."

The Rebirth Of Babylon

In the arid lands of the east, Babylon rose from the ashes of Human settlements. Here, the Venomous Elite ruled with a subtler hand, blending manipulation with brute force. Babylon's towering ziggurats, adorned with serpentine carvings, symbolized the supposed divinity of the serpent gods.

The city was a hub of trade, with captured Humans forced to craft goods and weapons that the lizardkin used to maintain their dominance. The Venomous Elite ensured that rumors of divine retribution kept the Human population in check.

Yet, even in captivity, the Humans whispered of their new god - the sun deity who represented love, understanding, and omnipotence. Kaelyss, one of the Venomous overseers of Babylon, dismissed these beliefs as irrelevant. "Let them follow their sun," she sneered. "Its light cannot reach beneath the earth."

But the whispers persisted, growing louder with each generation.

V-KAR'S EPIC

The Secrets Of Mu

Far across the seas, in the land of Mu, the lizardkin's grip was strongest. The Venomous Elite here were less divided, their unity forged by isolation and the harsh environment. Mu's fortress, perched atop a volcanic island, was impenetrable, its natural defenses augmented by the lizardkin's engineering.

Mu became the center of lizardkin experimentation, where scientists worked in secret to perfect the next generation of dragon-blooded warriors. Though the dragons remained in hibernation in the icy mountains, the lizardkin had not abandoned their dream of flight.

The Human slaves of Mu, like those in Atlantis and Babylon, clung to their faith. Unlike their eastern counterparts, they blended their sun-worship with the old serpent myths, creating a hybrid belief system that confused and frustrated their overseers.

"We cannot control them as we once did," said Drakess, one of Mu's leading scientists. "Their minds are evolving faster than their bodies."

Kwekwe, visiting Mu for a rare inspection, responded coldly. "Then control their bodies. Faith can only take them so far."

The Lizardfolk's Underground Empire

Beneath the surface, the lizardkin worked to consolidate their subterranean power. The mines beneath the great pyramid of V-Kar remained the lifeblood of their civilization, producing the resources needed to maintain their surface strongholds.

The Titans, though fewer in number after their reckless campaigns, continued to serve as enforcers, patrolling the tunnels and ensuring the laborers remained subjugated.

Wigwas, ever pragmatic, kept a close eye on the surface. "Atlantis, Babylon, and Mu are ours," she said during a council meeting. "But they are only as strong as the Humans beneath them are weak. Do not let them grow bold."

Faith In The Depths

Among the Human captives, the faith in the serpent god persisted, even underground. They whispered prayers as they toiled in the mines, their voices echoing through the dark. These prayers spoke not of fear, but of love - an unshakable belief in a god that understood their pain and would one day deliver them.

Kwekwe, observing the Humans in Atlantis, began to see the danger. "Their god gives them hope," she warned Wigwas during one of their meetings. "Hope is a seed that grows in silence. We must crush it before it blooms."

Wigwas, ever calculating, replied, "No. Let them hope. It blinds them to the reality of their chains. When the time comes, their faith will be their undoing."

V-KAR'S EPIC

The Return Of The Sun

Above the surface, the hominids' sun-worship spread like wildfire. The faith in the sun god, now fully developed, united the scattered Human tribes and kingdoms under a common purpose. This god, as they believed, was all-loving, all-knowing, and all-powerful - a beacon of light against the darkness of the lizardkin's reign.

For the lizardkin, the sun-worship presented a new challenge. The Humans no longer viewed the serpent gods with reverence or fear. To them, the serpents were false idols, usurpers of the true god's light.

In the cities of Atlantis, Babylon, and Mu, small uprisings began to stir. Though quickly crushed, these acts of defiance were a sign of the growing strength of the Humans' faith.

A Fragile Supremacy

As the lizardkin worked to maintain their hold on their surface strongholds, they began to realize the limits of their power. The dragons were gone, the Titans were dwindling, and the Venomous Elite were spread thin.

Kwekwe, standing atop the highest spire of Atlantis, gazed toward the horizon where the sun dipped below the sea. For the first time, she felt a flicker of unease.

"Faith," she whispered, her voice barely audible. "It is the one weapon we cannot break."

But beneath the surface, in the depths of the great pyramid, V-Kar slept on, undisturbed by the shifting tides of power. His people waited, their eyes ever turned toward the future, confident that when the time came, their Hegemon would rise again to lead them to glory.

Chapter 30: The Lizardfolk Adapt

The lizardkin, though diminished from their former glory, were a race bred for survival. Their strongholds - Atlantis, Babylon, and Mu - stood firm as symbols of their supremacy, but cracks had begun to form in their foundation. The growing faith of the Humans in their sun god, their increasing defiance, and the dragons' absence all forced the lizardkin to reassess their strategies.

Wigwas, the ruler of the underground empire, summoned a council of the Venomous Elite and the remaining Titans within the depths of the great pyramid. The meeting was somber, the echoes of the distant mines a constant reminder of the laborers who toiled below.

A Grim Assessment

"We are no longer untouchable," Wigwas said, her voice sharp and commanding. "The Humans grow stronger, emboldened by their faith. The sun god they follow is not real, but its power over them is undeniable. Faith has united them as we once united ourselves."

Kwekwe, ever the pragmatist, nodded. "Their faith is a weapon. It spreads like venom in the veins of their societies, strengthening them while weakening our control. The uprisings in Babylon were no coincidence. We crushed them, but they will rise again."

Nimatowin, the leader of the Titans, growled low. "Let them rise. We will crush them as we have always done. Their fire is a spark. We are the storm."

Wigwas turned her golden eyes to him, unflinching. "And how long can we weather the storm? The Titans are fewer with each generation. The dragons are gone. The Venomous Elite are stretched thin. We must change, or we will fall."

A Shift In Strategy
Wigwas outlined her plan to adapt to the new reality.

The strongholds of Atlantis, Babylon, and Mu would be further fortified. The Titans would focus their efforts on expanding the underground defenses, creating deeper tunnels and hidden chambers to protect against Human incursions.

"We cannot rely on the surface alone," Wigwas said. "If the Humans breach our cities, they must find nothing but stone and death."

The Venomous Elite, already skilled in manipulation, were tasked with infiltrating Human societies more deeply. Instead of ruling through fear and brute force, they would work to destabilize the Humans from within.

Kwekwe took the lead on this initiative. "We will whisper in their ears," she said. "Turn them against one another, sow distrust in their sun god. Their unity is their strength; we will make it their weakness."

The scientists of Mu, long shunned but indispensable, were ordered to focus on developing new weapons and technologies. Experiments on captured Humans were ramped up, with an emphasis on discovering weaknesses that could be exploited.

Drakess, one of the leading scientists, proposed creating hybrid creatures using Human and lizardkin genetics. "If we cannot outnumber them," he said, "we will create soldiers who can."

The mines beneath the pyramid were producing less with each passing year. To ensure the longevity of their civilization, Wigwas ordered a rationing of resources and a focus on preserving what they already had.

Atlantis: The Jewel Of Subterfuge

Atlantis became the center of the lizardkin's infiltration efforts. The Venomous Elite disguised themselves as emissaries of the serpent gods, mingling among the Human population and spreading carefully crafted lies.

They planted seeds of doubt about the sun god's omnipotence, whispering tales of the serpent gods' enduring power and warning of their eventual return. These efforts caused fractures in Human societies, with some returning to the worship of the serpents while others became more zealous in their sun worship.

Kwekwe, watching from the shadows, smiled coldly. "Let them fight among themselves. Their faith will tear them apart."

V-KAR'S EPIC

Babylon: The Bastion Of Strength

In Babylon, the Titans took center stage. The city's ziggurats were reinforced with massive stone blocks, their interiors turned into fortresses that could withstand prolonged sieges.

The Humans in Babylon's mines labored endlessly under the watchful eyes of their lizardkin overseers. Nimatowin personally oversaw the training of a new generation of Titan enforcers, their massive frames ensuring the lizardkin's dominance over the surface.

"Let the Humans come," Nimatowin said. "They will break themselves against our walls."

Mu: The Heart Of Innovation

Mu, isolated and secure, became the lizardkin's center of experimentation. The scientists, protected by the Venomous Elite, pushed the boundaries of what was possible.

Drakess unveiled his latest creation: a hybrid soldier, larger and stronger than a Human but faster and more cunning than a Titan. Though still in its infancy, the project showed promise.

"These creatures will be the future of warfare," Drakess said during a council meeting in Mu. "They will obey without question, and they will destroy without mercy."

Wigwas, though skeptical, allowed the project to continue. "If it succeeds, we will have an advantage. If it fails, we will have lost nothing."

Maintaining Supremacy

The lizardkin's efforts to adapt began to show results. The uprisings in Babylon and Atlantis were quelled with brutal efficiency, and the hybrid experiments in Mu hinted at a future where the lizardkin could regain their dominance.

But Wigwas knew their supremacy was fragile. The Humans' faith in their sun god continued to grow, and their ingenuity showed no signs of slowing.

As she stood in the great council chamber beneath the pyramid, Wigwas gazed at the dormant form of V-Kar, her thoughts heavy.

"We hold the surface by a thread," she murmured to herself. "But the thread is enough. For now."

A Growing Threat

Above the surface, the Humans continued to rebuild. Their sun-worship unified them in ways the lizardkin had never anticipated, and their technological advancements hinted at a future where they might challenge the lizardkin's remaining strongholds.

The Venomous Elite worked tirelessly to disrupt this progress, but even Kwekwe could not ignore the growing strength of the Human kingdoms.

"We cannot delay forever," Kwekwe warned Wigwas during a private meeting. "The Humans are learning. Soon, even our whispers will not be enough to stop them."

Wigwas's golden eyes narrowed. "Then we must be ready to meet them in the open. The day will come when the dragons rise again, and the earth will tremble beneath our claws. Until then, we hold, and we adapt."

Chapter 31: The Truth Behind Atlantis And Mu

As the lizardkin continued to adapt to their precarious dominance, their strongholds of Atlantis and Mu became deeply intertwined with the myths and history of the surface world. While the Venomous Elite operated in secret and the Titans ensured physical control, Wigwas and her council understood that shaping Human perception was their greatest weapon.

By embedding their influence into the very fabric of Human civilization, they ensured their presence would persist through legend, even as their physical dominance waned.

Atlantis: A City Of Wonder And Deception

Atlantis stood as the jewel of the lizardkin's surface empire, its location chosen for both strategic and symbolic reasons. Built on a vast island plateau surrounded by concentric canals, the city dazzled with its advanced architecture and abundant resources.

The Humans who lived under lizardkin rule in Atlantis were carefully managed. Most were kept in the fields and mines, their labor powering the city's grandeur. A select few, however, were allowed within the inner city, where the lizardkin presented themselves as divine overseers of a utopian society.

V-KAR'S EPIC

The Atlantis Experiment

Kwekwe and her agents used Atlantis as a proving ground for a new strategy: rather than rule solely through fear, they sought to create a society where Humans willingly served, believing they were part of something greater.

To this end, the lizardkin cultivated a narrative of divine enlightenment. The Venomous Elite, posing as emissaries of the serpent gods, taught Humans rudimentary engineering, navigation, and agriculture, presenting these advancements as gifts from their gods.

The result was a flourishing Human society that marveled at its own progress, oblivious to the manipulation behind it.

But Kwekwe remained wary. "This balance is fragile," she warned Wigwas. "The Humans believe we are benevolent because we allow them to believe it. One spark of rebellion, and they will see us for what we are."

The Downfall Of Atlantis

Despite its splendor, the foundations of Atlantis were inherently unstable. The lizardkin's mining operations beneath the island weakened its structure over time, and volcanic activity in the region further eroded its stability.

When a powerful earthquake struck, the island began to sink beneath the sea. Wigwas, unwilling to risk their strongest surface stronghold, ordered an evacuation. The lizardkin retreated to their subterranean sanctuaries, leaving the Human population to its fate.

V-KAR'S EPIC

The survivors of Atlantis carried its story across the ancient world, spreading tales of a magnificent city lost to the depths. To them, it became a cautionary tale of divine punishment or natural disaster - a myth that persisted for millennia.

For the lizardkin, Atlantis became a symbol of their failed experiment. "We gave them a glimpse of power," Kwekwe said bitterly, "and it destroyed them - and nearly us."

Mu: The Hidden Stronghold
Far across the oceans, in the vast reaches of the Pacific, Mu remained the most secure of the lizardkin's strongholds. Unlike Atlantis, which operated in the open, Mu was shrouded in secrecy. Its location atop a volcanic island allowed the lizardkin to maintain complete control over its environment.

The Humans of Mu lived in tightly controlled isolation. They knew nothing of the outside world, their lives entirely dictated by the lizardkin's experiments.

The Scientists Of Mu
Drakess and his team of scientists viewed Mu as a blank canvas for their work. Here, the lizardkin conducted experiments that would have been impossible in the more populated strongholds.

Among their projects were:

Hybrid Soldiers: Using captured Humans and dragon-blooded DNA, the scientists sought to create a new breed of warriors. These hybrids were stronger and faster than Humans but retained their adaptability and intelligence. Early prototypes were unstable, but progress was steady.

Bioengineering: The lizardkin experimented with enhancing their own biology, seeking to replicate the dragons' ability to fly and the Titans' immense strength.

Environmental Manipulation: Mu's volcanic environment provided a natural laboratory for testing geothermal energy and advanced mining techniques.

Drakess, presenting his findings to Wigwas during a rare visit, was cautiously optimistic. "We are close to breakthroughs that could secure our supremacy," he said. "But the work requires time - and secrecy."

Legends Of Mu

The Humans who escaped Mu - few as they were - brought with them fragmented memories of a mysterious land ruled by serpent gods. These tales spread among seafaring cultures, blending with myths of Atlantis to create enduring legends of a sunken paradise.

For the lizardkin, Mu remained a bastion of hope. Its isolation protected it from Human encroachment, and its experiments held the promise of a future where the lizardkin could regain their dominance.

V-KAR'S EPIC

The Growing Threat Of The Sun-Worshippers

While Atlantis and Mu remained critical to the lizardkin's plans, the rise of the sun-worshipping Humans posed an ever-increasing threat. United under their belief in an all-loving, all-knowing god, these Humans built kingdoms and armies that began to rival the lizardkin's remaining surface power.

In Babylon, Human slaves whispered of a coming reckoning, a time when the sun god would cast out the darkness and restore balance to the world. These whispers reached even the lizardkin overseers, unsettling them.

"Their faith is a flame," Nimatowin growled during a council meeting. "It burns brighter with each defeat. We must extinguish it before it consumes us."

But Wigwas, ever calculating, saw an opportunity. "Let them cling to their sun," she said. "We will shroud it in shadow. Fear is our weapon, and they will wield it against themselves."

A Fragile Supremacy

As the lizardkin worked to maintain their control, they could not ignore the cracks in their empire. Atlantis was gone, Mu remained isolated, and Babylon was a powder keg of unrest. The Humans, though scattered, were growing stronger with each passing generation.

In the depths of the great pyramid, Wigwas stood before the slumbering form of V-Kar. Her golden eyes gleamed with determination.

"We will hold the surface," she said softly. "We will adapt. And when you awaken, Hegemon, the world will tremble once more."

Chapter 32: Shadows Of The Ice

The earth shifted, plunging into an age of ice. Snow blanketed the lands, and glaciers crept across the continents, transforming lush valleys and fertile plains into barren, frozen wastelands. For the lizardkin, this was a cataclysm unlike any they had faced before. Cold-blooded and unable to generate their own warmth, they retreated into their subterranean sanctuaries, their strongholds beneath Atlantis, Babylon, and Mu sealed off as they entered a collective hibernation.

Above the surface, the Humans adapted. Their ingenuity allowed them to survive the bitter cold, crafting clothing from animal hides and building shelters to protect against the freezing winds. Fire became their lifeblood, a symbol of their endurance.

But as the ice age slowly came to an end, the lizardkin awoke to a world they no longer recognized.

Awakening To Horror

The lizardkin emerged from their long slumber to find the earth irrevocably changed. The glaciers had receded, revealing a scarred landscape. The great forests of old were gone, replaced by vast, desolate plains. The Humans, far from being weakened by the ice age, had flourished. Their numbers had multiplied, and their societies had advanced in ways the lizardkin could scarcely comprehend.

In the depths of Mu, Drakess was one of the first to awaken. He observed the surface world through stolen glimpses, using Human captives and crude observational devices to gather information. What he saw filled him with dread.

"They have discovered fire that rivals the sun," Drakess reported during an emergency council meeting in Babylon. "Their weapons can obliterate entire cities in an instant. I have seen the ruins of such destruction with my own eyes. They call it Greek."

The council fell silent, their fear palpable.

A New Strategy

Wigwas, ever pragmatic, took control of the situation. "We cannot face them openly," she said. "The Humans have become a species of war. They are reckless, destructive, and dangerous beyond anything we imagined. If we are to survive, we must adapt once more."

She outlined a plan to retreat further into the shadows, to observe and manipulate from afar rather than engage directly.

Myths Of Fear

To keep the Humans wary of the unknown, the lizardkin began to seed myths and legends into Human culture. They whispered tales of vampires, creatures that drank the blood of the living, and lycanthropes, beasts that hunted under the full moon.

"Let them fear the shadows," Kwekwe said with a cold smile. "Let them believe the night belongs to monsters."

V-KAR'S EPIC

Underground Expansion
The lizardkin focused on expanding their subterranean networks, creating vast hidden cities and sanctuaries far beneath the earth's surface. These new strongholds were designed to be impenetrable, ensuring the lizardkin could remain hidden from Human detection.

Observation And Intelligence
Spies and Venomous Elite infiltrated Human societies, blending into the shadows to gather information. The lizardkin sought to understand the Humans' technology, their weaknesses, and their growing faith in both science and religion.

The Obsidian Globe
One day, deep beneath the ruins of Atlantis, a Venomous scout returned from an expedition with a strange artifact: an obsidian globe, its surface etched with ancient, glowing runic symbols. The artifact radiated an energy unlike anything the lizardkin had encountered before.

The globe was brought to Wigwas, who examined it with growing unease. "This is not Human," she said. "Nor is it of our making. What is this?"

Drakess, summoned from Mu to study the artifact, was equally baffled. "The runes are similar to those found in our oldest sanctuaries," he said. "But they predate even our records. I cannot decipher them."

Kwekwe, ever suspicious, voiced what many were thinking. "If it is not Human, and it is not ours, then who left it for us? And why?"

A Message In The Shadows

The Venomous scout who delivered the globe claimed to have found it in a Human black market, where it was being sold as a curiosity. The Humans, it seemed, had no idea of its true significance. But the fact that it had been left unguarded, and that it had found its way into the lizardkin's hands, suggested intent.

Wigwas ordered the globe to be studied in secret, its existence kept hidden even from most of the council. "Whatever this is," she said, "it was meant to find us. Until we understand its purpose, it will remain our greatest secret."

The Lizardfolk's Growing Paranoia

The discovery of the globe only deepened the lizardkin's paranoia. Already wary of the Humans' destructive potential, they now faced the unsettling possibility of an unknown third party working in the shadows.

To ensure their survival, the lizardkin redoubled their efforts to manipulate Human myths. The legends of vampires and werewolves became more pervasive, spread through whispers and symbols planted in Human culture.

Kwekwe personally oversaw the creation of elaborate rituals designed to reinforce these myths. "If the Humans fear the shadows," she said, "they will never look too closely at what hides within them."

A World Forever Changed

As the lizardkin adapted to the new world, they realized that their time of open dominance had passed. The Humans had become a force too powerful to confront directly. But in the darkness, the lizardkin remained, watching, waiting, and weaving their influence into the fabric of Human society.

And in the depths of their hidden sanctuaries, the obsidian globe pulsed faintly, its runes glowing like distant stars.

Chapter 33: Secrets Of The Obsidian Globe

The obsidian globe, covered in glowing runes and radiating an enigmatic energy, had become an object of both fascination and dread within the lizardkin's hidden empire. Wigwas had entrusted its study to Drakess, the most brilliant and cautious of their scientists, who worked tirelessly in the depths of Mu to uncover its secrets.

At the same time, Kwekwe and the Venomous Elite intensified their efforts to embed the myths of vampires and lycanthropes into Human culture. The combination of fear and distraction ensured that Humans would never question what might truly be hiding in the shadows.

Drakess's Discovery

Deep beneath Mu, Drakess and his team worked in silence. The laboratory was filled with the hum of strange devices, scavenged and modified from both lizardkin and Human technology. The globe sat on a raised pedestal, its runes flickering faintly as if responding to unseen forces.

Drakess meticulously cataloged its properties:

Material: The globe was made of pure obsidian, but its surface was unnaturally smooth, as if shaped by forces beyond physical tools.

Energy Field: It emitted a faint but consistent energy, neither heat nor light, that seemed to interact with its surroundings. Nearby devices sometimes sparked unpredictably.

"They are unaware," Drakess assured her. "Their focus remains on their wars and their gods. But if they were to discover this…"

"They must not," Wigwas said firmly. "Begin preparations to investigate the site. And ensure that no trace of this reaches Human eyes."

The Globe's Purpose

The globe's true purpose remained elusive, but its implications were clear: the lizardkin were not alone. The knowledge it contained could change everything, but it also posed a grave risk.

Wigwas convened a secret council with Kwekwe, Drakess, and Nimatowin to discuss the next steps.

"We face threats from above and below," Wigwas said. "The Humans grow stronger with each passing year, and now we must consider the possibility of others - beings who may see us as we see the Humans."

Kwekwe nodded. "If this globe is a warning, we must heed it. If it is a tool, we must wield it."

The Shadows Deepen

As the lizardkin prepared to send an expedition to the Antarctic, they intensified their efforts to control the surface world through myth and manipulation. Humans continued to fear the dark, the shadows, and the creatures they believed lurked within.

Runes: The symbols etched into its surface bore a resemblance to the ancient lizardkin language but were more intricate, layered with meanings Drakess could only partially grasp.

After weeks of study, a breakthrough occurred. When exposed to certain sound frequencies - specifically those mimicking the growls and hisses of the lizardkin - the runes began to shift, rearranging themselves. Drakess recorded the phenomenon, his claws trembling as the runes formed a pattern resembling a star map.

"These are not random symbols," Drakess muttered to himself. "They are coordinates."

A Message From The Stars

As Drakess and his team delved deeper, they uncovered an unsettling truth: the globe was not of earthly origin. The energy it emitted, the complexity of its design, and the alignment of the star map suggested it had come from beyond the planet.

Drakess presented his findings to Wigwas and the council in Babylon. "This globe is a message," he said. "A signal, perhaps even a warning. Whoever created it knew of us. They may still be watching."

The council was divided. Kwekwe argued for caution, suggesting the globe be hidden or destroyed. "If this is a weapon or a trap, we should not let it endanger us," she said.

Wigwas, however, saw opportunity. "If this is knowledge from beyond, it could be the key to our survival. We must understand it fully before we decide its fate."

Whispers In The Shadows

While Drakess studied the globe, Kwekwe turned her attention to the Humans. The myths of vampires and lycanthropes had already begun to take root, but she sought to weave them deeper into the Human psyche.

The Venomous Elite planted stories of pale, immortal beings that drank the blood of the living. These creatures were said to dwell in ancient castles and avoid sunlight - legends carefully crafted to keep Humans from investigating the lizardkin's hidden sanctuaries.

Human captives released into the world spread these stories unknowingly, their fear fueling the myths.

Drawing inspiration from their own Berserker kin, the lizardkin spread tales of shapeshifters - Humans who transformed into beasts under the full moon. The Venomous Elite ensured these stories were tied to remote forests and caves, areas where lizardkin activity was most concentrated.

"The more they fear the dark," Kwekwe said to her agents, "the less they will question what lurks within it."

V-KAR'S EPIC

Human Superstition Takes Hold

The myths spread quickly, embedded in the oral traditions of Human societies. Peasants told stories of shadowy figures stalking the night, and kings commissioned hunts for beasts that roamed their forests. Fear of the unknown became a defining trait of Human culture, ensuring that the lizardkin's presence remained concealed.

In the growing urban centers of Europe, rumors of vampires in the castles of the Carpathian Mountains became widespread. Meanwhile, in the Americas, settlers whispered of strange creatures howling in the wilderness, their cries echoing through the night.

The lizardkin watched from the shadows, satisfied that their manipulation was working.

A Second Revelation

Months after the initial discovery, Drakess made another breakthrough with the obsidian globe. By combining the star map with ancient texts recovered from Mu, he realized the coordinates pointed to a specific region on Earth - an area beneath the Antarctic ice.

"This is no mere message," Drakess told Wigwas during a private meeting. "It is a guide. Whatever lies beneath the ice may hold the answers to our origins - or our future."

Wigwas's expression remained unreadable. "And you are certain the Humans do not know of this?"

And beneath the surface, the obsidian globe pulsed faintly, its runes shifting in patterns that no lizardkin could yet understand.

Chapter 34: The Antarctic Expedition And Myths Of The Shadows

Deep in the subterranean sanctuaries of Mu, preparations for the Antarctic expedition were underway. The obsidian globe, pulsing faintly, had revealed its secrets to Drakess - coordinates pointing to a location far beneath the Antarctic ice sheet. Wigwas's command was clear: uncover whatever lay there before the Humans could even dream of its existence.

The journey would be treacherous. The lizardkin, cold-blooded by nature, were ill-suited to the freezing conditions of the polar regions. Only a small team of the most adaptable Venomous Elite, led by Kaelyss, was chosen for the mission. They carried specialized thermal gear developed in Mu's laboratories and provisions to sustain them through the harsh environment.

The Expedition Begins

Kaelyss and her team emerged from a hidden coastal outpost, navigating through a labyrinth of tunnels that opened onto the Antarctic shoreline. The howling winds cut through their scales like knives, but their thermal cloaks, laced with bioengineered fibers, provided enough warmth to survive.

Their goal was a precise location marked on the star map etched into the globe - a point deep beneath the ice, accessible only by descending through a natural fissure.

Drakess's final words to Kaelyss echoed in her mind: "If you find anything, do not awaken it until you are certain it cannot awaken you first."

Beneath The Ice

After days of grueling travel, the team reached the fissure. Kaelyss gazed down into the abyss, the glowing runes on the globe faintly illuminating the icy walls. They descended slowly, their claws finding purchase on the jagged surfaces.

At the bottom of the fissure lay a cavern of crystalline ice, its walls shimmering with an unnatural glow. In the center stood a massive structure - a perfect black obelisk, its surface carved with runes identical to those on the globe.

Kaelyss approached cautiously, the globe in her claws. As she drew near, the runes on both the globe and the obelisk began to shift, aligning with one another in a sequence that seemed almost alive.

"This is not of this earth," Kaelyss whispered. "It predates even us."

The Myths Take Root

While the expedition delved into the mysteries beneath the ice, Kwekwe and the Venomous Elite continued their work on the surface. Human culture, fractured yet flourishing, was ripe for manipulation. The myths of vampires and lycanthropes became more than stories - they became deeply ingrained beliefs.

In the heart of Europe, rumors of vampires spread like wildfire. The Venomous Elite, using their natural stealth and cunning, played into these fears by appearing only at night, their scales gleaming faintly in the moonlight.

They targeted isolated villages, draining livestock and leaving the Humans to believe they were preyed upon by immortal, blood-drinking monsters.

Kwekwe personally oversaw the creation of false "vampire lairs," hidden chambers filled with Human bones and crude symbols meant to terrify any who stumbled upon them.

"We are the shadows," Kwekwe said to her agents. "Let them believe we are everywhere, and they will never dare to look too closely."

In the Americas and the forests of Eurasia, the myths of lycanthropes - Humans who transformed into beasts - took hold. The Venomous Elite encouraged these stories by releasing Berserkers into the wild under the light of the full moon.

The Berserkers, their bloodlust barely contained, would wreak havoc on small settlements before retreating into the woods. Survivors spread tales of monstrous wolves with glowing eyes and unearthly strength.

"These myths protect us," Kwekwe explained to Wigwas during a council meeting. "They keep Humans afraid of the dark and the wilderness. As long as they fear, they will not venture too far into the shadows."

V-KAR'S EPIC

The Obelisk Awakens

Back in Antarctica, Kaelyss and her team discovered that the obelisk was not merely a monument - it was a machine. As the runes aligned, the obelisk began to hum with a low, resonant frequency.

The glow intensified, illuminating the cavern with an eerie, otherworldly light. A series of images flashed across the surface of the obelisk, showing glimpses of star systems, unfamiliar landscapes, and strange, towering figures.

"What is this?" one of the Venomous agents whispered, their voice trembling.

Kaelyss stepped back, clutching the globe tightly. "A record," she said, her voice filled with awe and fear. "A memory of something far older than us."

The images faded, replaced by a single symbol that pulsed steadily - a spiral of interlocking runes that seemed to beckon them closer.

A Warning Unheeded

Drakess's warning echoed in Kaelyss's mind, but curiosity overwhelmed her caution. She reached out, pressing the globe against the obelisk. The runes flared brightly, and the cavern trembled as a voice, deep and resonant, filled the air.

"They will awaken. The cycle begins anew."

The glow dimmed, and the obelisk fell silent once more. Kaelyss staggered back, her claws shaking.

"We need to leave," she said, her voice barely above a whisper. "Now."

<u>A World In Fear</u>

As Kaelyss and her team began their return journey, the myths on the surface continued to grow. The Humans, now entrenched in their beliefs, built entire societies around their fear of the unknown. Vampires and lycanthropes became symbols of caution, their legends discouraging exploration of dark places and wild lands.

The lizardkin watched from the shadows, satisfied that their manipulation was working. But beneath their satisfaction lay an unspoken fear - fear of the obelisk, the globe, and the ominous message it had delivered.

Chapter 35: The Orb's True Purpose

Back in the depths of Mu, the obsidian globe now held a far more ominous weight. The warning Kaelyss had triggered at the Antarctic obelisk - "They will awaken. The cycle begins anew." - spread unease among the lizardkin council. The globe, once a mere curiosity, was now a symbol of impending danger.

Wigwas ordered it moved to a fortified chamber deep beneath Mu, accessible only to Drakess and a select few scientists. No one else was to approach it without her express permission.

"It is no longer an artifact," Wigwas declared to the council. "It is a weapon, a key, or a threat. Until we understand it fully, we remain blind to what lies ahead."

Drakess's Continued Study

Within the reinforced chamber, Drakess and his team resumed their research, this time with heightened urgency. The globe's surface, constantly shifting with faint runes, seemed more alive than before.

Drakess's first task was to decipher the recurring spiral symbol that had appeared on the Antarctic obelisk. Using fragments of ancient lizardkin texts recovered from Mu, he began to piece together a meaning:

The Spiral: Represented a repeating cycle, possibly one of destruction and renewal. It suggested that whatever was coming had happened before - and would happen again.

The Runic Alignments: The runes shifted based on environmental factors, particularly sound frequencies and proximity to specific materials, including obsidian and iron.

The Energy Field: The globe emitted a subtle magnetic pulse, which fluctuated when exposed to starlight. Drakess theorized that it might react differently under certain celestial alignments.

"This is no ordinary device," Drakess explained to Wigwas during a private report. "It seems to be a transmitter, a receiver, and perhaps even a repository of knowledge. But its creators… they are far beyond anything we understand."

Unlocking The Spiral

One breakthrough came when Drakess exposed the globe to sound frequencies mimicking those emitted by the obelisk. The runes rearranged themselves into a new configuration, forming what appeared to be a map.

The map depicted not just Earth, but other celestial bodies as well - planets, moons, and distant stars, all connected by a network of spiraling paths. At the center of the map was a single glowing symbol, larger and more intricate than the others.

"This must be their origin," Drakess murmured, his claws tracing the glowing pattern. "The place where they first awakened."

V-KAR'S EPIC

A Forgotten Race

Further analysis revealed fragments of data embedded within the runes. These fragments suggested that the creators of the globe - whom Drakess began to refer to as "the Architects" - were an ancient and highly advanced species.

The Architects had left behind structures and devices across the galaxy, each one tied to the spiral network depicted on the globe. The Antarctic obelisk was merely one such device, designed to monitor and possibly influence the development of life on Earth.

"But why leave it for us?" Wigwas asked during a council meeting. "Why would they care what happens to this world?"

Drakess hesitated before replying. "Perhaps we were meant to find it. Or perhaps we weren't. Either way, it seems to be part of a larger plan - one we cannot yet comprehend."

A Grim Revelation

As Drakess delved deeper, the globe began to react more strongly to his presence. The runes glowed brighter, and the magnetic pulse intensified. It was as if the device were alive, responding to his efforts to uncover its secrets.

Then, one night, the globe activated on its own. The runes aligned into a single, coherent script, one that filled the chamber with a blinding light.

Drakess and his team recoiled as a voice, low and resonant, filled the air:

"The Watchers slumber, but their gaze never fades. The cycle will end, but only through fire. Prepare yourselves, for the Architects return to reclaim what was theirs."

The light faded, and the globe fell silent once more.

The Council's Debate

Drakess reported the message to the council, sparking heated debate.

Kwekwe, ever cautious, was the first to speak. "This is a warning, plain and simple. If the Architects are returning, we must prepare for war - or extinction."

Nimatowin growled in agreement. "Let them come. If they want this world, they'll have to fight us for it."

Wigwas, however, took a more measured approach. "We do not know their intentions," she said. "If they are as advanced as this globe suggests, open conflict would be suicide. We must learn more before we act."

A Risky Experiment

Drakess proposed a daring plan: to activate the globe fully and attempt direct communication with the Architects.

"This device is a beacon," he explained. "It is meant to be found and used. If we can understand their purpose, we may find a way to avoid destruction - or perhaps even gain their favor."

Wigwas hesitated. The risks were immense, but the alternative - remaining in ignorance - was equally dangerous.

"Proceed," she said finally. "But do so in secret. If this fails, no one must know."

The Globe's Activation

In the deepest chamber of Mu, Drakess and his team prepared for the experiment. The globe was placed at the center of a runic circle, surrounded by devices designed to amplify its energy field.

When the signal was activated, the chamber filled with an overwhelming light. The runes on the globe shifted rapidly, forming patterns too complex for even Drakess to follow.

Then, as the light dimmed, an image appeared - a holographic figure, tall and slender, with elongated limbs and glowing, featureless eyes.

The figure spoke, its voice calm yet powerful:

"You have awakened the beacon. The Watchers will know. Your actions have begun the final cycle. Prepare yourselves, for the Architects return with neither mercy nor malice."

The image faded, leaving the chamber in silence.

<u>The Final Cycle Begins</u>

Drakess emerged from the chamber visibly shaken. "The Architects are coming," he told Wigwas. "We don't know when or why, but their return is inevitable."

Wigwas, though outwardly calm, felt a rare pang of fear. "Then we must prepare," she said. "Not just for them, but for the Humans as well. This world is ours, and we will not give it up without a fight."

As the council dispersed, the obsidian globe sat silently in its chamber, its runes shifting faintly as if watching, waiting.

Chapter 36: The Rebels' Ripple and the Awakening of V-Kar

The obsidian globe pulsed violently within the depths of Mu, its energy field growing unstable. Drakess and his team scrambled to contain it, but the intensity of the reaction exceeded anything they had seen before.

Across the vast underground network of the lizardkin, the very earth seemed to tremble. Those closest to the globe described a sense of distortion - a pulling sensation, as if time itself was warping.

And then, it happened.

In a burst of searing light, the globe split its focus. Its twin - a second identical orb - momentarily appeared out of nothingness in Mu before vanishing just as abruptly, leaving the chamber in stunned silence. Drakess, still clutching the first globe, felt his body twist unnaturally as the artifact's impossible proximity activated a unique mechanism: it tore through the temporal fabric and flung Drakess back through time.

The Arrival In 5000 BC

Through careful navigation and the use of his innate stealth, Drakess made his way to the lizardfolk's ancient sanctuaries.

He quickly realized something was terribly wrong. The air felt different, the stars overhead unfamiliar. The planet itself seemed younger, fresher. He had been thrown into the past - exactly equidistant from the "center of time," as determined by the globe's mechanisms.

Steeling himself, Drakess formulated his priority: the orb must be delivered to the hegemonal city to ensure it would survive until the present day, ready for V-Kar's eventual awakening.

Delivering the Orb to the Hegemonal City

Through careful navigation and the use of his innate stealth, Drakess made his way to what remained of the lizardkin's ancient sanctuaries. The ruins of the once-great hegemonal city lay dormant, long abandoned but still holding echoes of their former glory.

Drakess concealed the orb deep within the most secure chamber, leaving etched instructions in an ancient lizardkin dialect for the future generation who would awaken V-Kar. His instructions were clear:

V-KAR'S EPIC

The Globe's Use: The orb was to be activated only in the presence of the hegemon, who would interpret its message and devise a strategy for its purpose.

The Timing: The orb must align with specific celestial configurations to maximize its influence.

The New Plan: The future hegemon must rewrite Human history to move the center of time forward, ensuring lizardkin supremacy in the face of growing Human strength.

The Awakening Of V-Kar

In the present era of the lizardkin's underground empire, the reverberations of the Architects' arrival reached far and wide. The proximity of the two orbs had activated latent mechanisms within the lizardkin's subterranean network, sending powerful energy pulses through the chambers beneath the great pyramid.

Wigwas and the council, realizing the significance of the event, unanimously decided to awaken V-Kar earlier than planned. The slumbering hegemon, encased in a crystalline sarcophagus, stirred as the activation sequences completed.

V-Kar's golden eyes opened, their piercing gaze sweeping the chamber. He stepped forward, his massive frame exuding authority.

"Why have I been woken?" he growled.

V-KAR'S EPIC

Wigwas bowed low. "Great Hegemon, the orb has spoken. The Architects' ripple through time has begun. We need your wisdom to guide us through this new challenge."

V-Kar studied the orb, its runes glowing faintly in his clawed hand. The knowledge it radiated filled his mind with glimpses of the past, present, and future. He saw the ripple of the Architects' influence as they moved closer to the center of time, their power growing and waning in tandem with their temporal proximity.

"This is no ordinary tool," V-Kar said, his voice heavy with revelation. "It is a key - a weapon of time itself. We must act swiftly."

The Rewriting Of The Mayan Calendar
V-Kar's first directive was bold: to move the center of time forward to 2012 AD, a point of immense significance in Human history. He understood that by influencing the ancient Mayan civilization, he could set the groundwork for a global shift in Human perception - one that would ensure the lizardkin's long-term supremacy.

The instructions etched by Drakess centuries earlier included references to the Mayan calendar. Using the orb as a focal point, V-Kar and his scholars deciphered the ancient glyphs, reconfiguring the calendar's predictions to align with a pivotal event: the year 2012, a moment that Humans would later interpret as the "end of the world."

"This date will become a nexus of fear and hope," V-Kar explained to the council. "Humans will obsess over it, distracted by their superstitions. Meanwhile, we will use their chaos to ensure our own survival."

Implementing The Plan

Using the orb's mechanisms, V-Kar manipulated the temporal echoes embedded in the ancient Mayan glyphs. These subtle changes ensured that the calendar would predict a monumental shift in 2012.

The Venomous Elite were tasked with infiltrating Human societies, planting myths and legends about the Mayan prophecy. Stories of an impending apocalypse spread across cultures, creating a global sense of unease.

V-Kar envisioned a future where Humanity, paralyzed by its own fears, would be ripe for lizardkin domination. "We will rise when they falter," he declared. "And this time, we will not fall."

The Architects' Shadow

Despite his confidence, V-Kar could not ignore the looming presence of the Architects. The orb continued to pulse faintly, its energy field growing stronger as the rebels approached the center of time.

"They are not gods," V-Kar said during a council meeting. "But they are powerful. We must be prepared for their return - not as saviors, but as adversaries."

Wigwas nodded. "And the Humans?"

V-KAR'S EPIC

"They will destroy themselves," V-Kar replied, his golden eyes gleaming. "And we will ensure it."

Chapter 37: The Architects' Approach And The Fall Of V-Kar

As the temporal ripples of the Architects intensified, the lizardkin began to feel the weight of their impending arrival. The orb, once faint and mysterious, now pulsed with a frantic energy. Its runes shifted constantly, rearranging into sequences that none could decipher fully.

V-Kar, now fully awake and commanding his people with renewed vigor, recognized the Architects as a force growing stronger as they neared the center of time. These "Rebels" existed both in and outside time, their influence waxing as they approached their temporal zenith.

"This is no mere coincidence," V-Kar told the council. "They are drawn here as if by design. Their presence threatens everything we have built."

Contact In The Shadows

The first direct encounter with the Architects occurred in the ruins of Babylon. Kwekwe and a group of Venomous Elite had been dispatched to investigate reports of temporal disturbances, strange lights, and whispers from displaced Human tribes.

In the shadow of a crumbling ziggurat, the Venomous Elite found the remnants of an Architect beacon - its design eerily similar to the obsidian globe. The beacon thrummed with alien energy, and standing before it was a towering figure, partially translucent, its edges flickering like a mirage.

V-KAR'S EPIC

The figure turned toward them, its glowing eyes devoid of malice yet impossibly piercing. It spoke in a language that resonated more in thought than sound.

"You are outside your moment. Return, or be undone."

The Venomous Elite recoiled, their venom-tipped claws shaking. Kwekwe, ever brave, stepped forward. "We were here first," she hissed. "This world belongs to us."

The Architect paused, its presence expanding to fill the air like an unseen weight. "You exist because you were allowed to. But allowance is fleeting."

V-Kar's Stand

When news of the encounter reached V-Kar, he responded decisively. "We will not be undone by these so-called Architects," he declared. "If they seek to challenge us, we will show them the strength of the lizardkin."

He led a force of Berserkers and Titans to the site of the encounter, determined to destroy the beacon and drive the Architects from his world.

But as they arrived, the beacon flared with an overwhelming light. The orb in V-Kar's claws pulsed in response, the runes forming intricate spirals that seemed to connect to the beacon. For a brief moment, V-Kar's mind was flooded with visions - worlds collapsing, timelines fracturing, and the Architects' presence growing stronger with each step toward the center of time.

"Destroy it!" V-Kar roared, shaking off the visions.

The Berserkers charged, their claws tearing at the beacon's base. The Titans swung their massive fists, shattering its crystalline components. But as the beacon fell, the air itself seemed to rupture.

The Architects' Intervention
From the fractured beacon emerged three more of the translucent figures, their forms pulsing with temporal energy. The Architects, though non-corporeal, projected a force so immense that even the Titans hesitated.

One of the Architects extended a flickering limb toward V-Kar, and the orb in his hand reacted violently. Runes flared, blinding light engulfed the battlefield, and V-Kar felt himself pulled into a temporal vortex.

Before disappearing, he shouted one final order: "Preserve the city! Preserve our kind!"

The Temporal Displacement
V-Kar found himself hurled through time, the orb's energy guiding his journey. He landed in a barren desert, his body battered but alive. Around him, the world was eerily still, the sands whispering of centuries yet to pass.

The orb in his claws pulsed faintly, its runes now forming a single coherent message: "Hibernate. Survive. The time is not yet yours."

V-Kar, though reluctant, understood the directive. He dug deep into the sand, carving out a chamber where he could slumber undisturbed. "Another few centuries," he murmured. "When the time is right, I will rise again."

The Next Keeper Of The Orb
Back in the ruins of Babylon, the Venomous Elite retrieved the orb, now left behind by V-Kar's displacement. Kwekwe, shaken by the encounter with the Architects, chose one of her most trusted agents, Kaelyss, to guard it.

Kaelyss, holding the orb, felt its energy pulling her, just as it had done to V-Kar. Before the council could stop her, she too was drawn into a temporal vortex, hurled back through time to deliver a message that would alter the course of history.

The Message That Saves V-Kar
Kaelyss arrived centuries earlier, in the early days of the lizardkin empire. She used the orb to carve a message into the walls of an ancient sanctuary:

"To the Hegemon: When the Architects come, you must not fall. Hibernate where none can find you. Your time will come, but only if you wait. The cycle depends on it."

The sanctuary, buried and forgotten, would remain untouched until V-Kar's eventual awakening.

The Architects Retreat
As the Architects continued their approach toward the center of time, their presence waxed, their strength tied to

their temporal proximity. The Venomous Elite, recognizing this, worked to minimize their activity, retreating further into the shadows and preserving the lizardkin's remaining strongholds.

Wigwas, now leading in V-Kar's absence, declared, "The Hegemon will return. Until then, we endure. Let the Humans believe they rule. Their time is fleeting. Ours is eternal."

<u>A New Era Awaits</u>

The lizardkin, though fractured and diminished, began preparing for V-Kar's prophesied return. The orb, now hidden once more, pulsed faintly in its chamber, waiting for the moment when it would guide its master to rise again.

In the distance, the Architects moved ever closer to their final destination - a point in time where all would converge, and the cycle would begin anew.

Chapter 38: V-Kar's Second Awakening and the New Plan

The sands of time, shifting ever closer to chaos and entropy, finally brought V-Kar back into the light in the year 1930 AD. His chamber, buried deep beneath what had become a sprawling desert, cracked open with a low rumble. The orb he had left behind centuries earlier remained silent, its energy dormant until they got close enough to 2012.

As V-Kar emerged, his golden eyes scanned a world drastically different from the one he had left. The air was dense with the fumes of industry, the skies crisscrossed by

Human aircraft, and the ground vibrated with the relentless march of Human machines.

"They have grown far too bold," V-Kar growled, his voice resonating with disdain. "The Humans think themselves rulers of this world."

The Message From The Past
The sanctuary where Kaelyss had left her warning all those centuries ago was rediscovered by Kwekwe and the Venomous Elite. The message carved into the stone walls echoed through the lizardkin's council chambers as Wigwas read it aloud.

"To the Hegemon: When the Architects come, you must not fall. Hibernate where none can find you. Your time will come, but only if you wait. The cycle depends on it."

This message had saved V-Kar's life, allowing him to hibernate far from the battlefields of his first fall, but its implications were dire. The Architects' influence was waning as they receded into impossibility, yet the danger they represented had not vanished entirely. The timeline, fragile and malleable, had shifted once more, leaving the lizardkin in a precarious position.

The Lizardfolk's Hidden Empire
The lizardkin retreated into the shadows, their remaining strongholds hidden deep beneath the earth. The ruins of Babylon, the volcanic fortress of Mu, and the submerged remnants of Atlantis served as sanctuaries for their kind.

V-KAR'S EPIC

The Venomous Elite continued to manipulate Human myths, ensuring that stories of monsters, shadows, and ancient evils persisted in the Human psyche. But they knew that myths alone would no longer suffice.

Wigwas welcomed V-Kar back with a reverence born of desperation. "Hegemon," she said, bowing low, "the Humans grow stronger every year. Their weapons can wipe out entire cities. Their reach extends to the skies and beyond. We need a plan."

Plan A: The Last Dragon

V-Kar's gaze shifted to the Berserkers, now reduced to a dwindling few. Among them was Akuaq's progeny, a massive, dragon-blooded creature named Tunngasuaq, said to be the strongest of his kind. Tunngasuaq's wings stretched wider than any before him, his fire burned hotter, and his ferocity was unmatched.

V-Kar saw in him a weapon - a being who could bring the full wrath of the lizardkin upon Humanity.

"We will send Tunngasuaq," V-Kar declared to the council. "One dragon, the most powerful to ever live. He will be sent back to the ancient past to raze their civilizations before they can rise. Let them never see the light of progress. Let their story end before it begins."

The council erupted in murmurs. Wigwas stepped forward. "But the orb remains dormant until 2002. We cannot manipulate the timeline without it."

V-Kar's jaw tightened. "Then we prepare. When the orb reawakens, Tunngasuaq will travel back through time and end Humanity before it begins. Until then, we remain hidden."

Plan B: The Final Message

While Plan A focused on preventing Humanity's rise, Plan B was even more devastating. V-Kar, ever the strategist, devised a contingency: a final message to be sent back in time if Tunngasuaq failed.

This message, encoded in the orb's runes, would be an instruction to their past selves: unleash everything. The lizardkin of the ancient timeline would be directed to focus their efforts on eradicating Humanity at all costs, sacrificing their own future to ensure Humanity's destruction.

"This is not a plan we undertake lightly," V-Kar said, addressing the council. "It is a last resort, one that will destroy not only Humanity but the timeline itself. If Plan B is executed, there will be nothing left - no Humans, no lizardkin, only entropy."

Preparing The Dragon

Tunngasuaq, already a towering figure of power, began an intense regimen of training. The lizardkin scientists in Mu enhanced his body further, strengthening his scales, increasing the intensity of his fire, and perfecting his ability to fly vast distances.

The Venomous Elite, meanwhile, worked to ensure that Tunngasuaq's mission would succeed. They studied Human history, identifying key points where the dragon's intervention would have the greatest impact.

"If he strikes before the rise of civilization, he can destroy their ability to organize," Kwekwe said. "If he targets their earliest cities, they will never advance."

V-Kar's Restlessness

Though V-Kar had a plan, he found himself increasingly restless. The Humans, now armed with weapons capable of leveling entire cities, posed an existential threat that could not be ignored.

In 1945, news reached the lizardkin of the atomic bombings of Hiroshima and Nagasaki. V-Kar stood in stunned silence as Wigwas recounted the devastation.

"They have harnessed fire greater than even Tunngasuaq's," she said grimly.

For the first time, V-Kar felt doubt creep into his mind. The Humans, so small and frail, had become the ultimate force of destruction.

"We must act quickly," he said finally. "The longer we wait, the stronger they become. We cannot allow their power to eclipse our own."

V-KAR'S EPIC

The Dormant Orb

The orb, though silent, remained a constant presence in V-Kar's plans. It sat in a reinforced chamber beneath Mu, its runes inactive yet pregnant with potential.

V-Kar often visited the chamber, his claws tracing the artifact's surface as he contemplated its power. He knew that when it reawakened in 2002, it would be the key to everything - the key to either their salvation or their annihilation.

"We will wait," V-Kar said to himself. "But when the time comes, we will strike with the fury of dragons and the wisdom of ages."

A Fragile Peace

For the next decades, the lizardkin remained hidden, their numbers dwindling but their resolve unbroken. They watched Humanity's rise with a mix of awe and hatred, knowing that their time would come again.

And deep within the earth, Tunngasuaq's wings stretched in anticipation, his fire simmering, his eyes locked on a future - or a past - where he would fulfill his destiny.

Chapter 39: The Dragon's Preparation And The Lizardfolk's Struggle

In the depths of Mu, Tunngasuaq stood at the heart of an expansive cavern illuminated by the glow of bioengineered crystals. His wings, large enough to blot out the cavern's light when spread, shimmered with reinforced scales. Each was layered with alloys forged in the volcanic heat of Mu's deepest chambers, giving him an unnatural resilience. His fire burned with the intensity of a star, the result of decades of enhancements by the lizardkin scientists.

Tunngasuaq had been crafted not only to be a weapon but to be an apocalypse - a creature capable of reducing the strongest of Human civilizations to ash.

Training For The Impossible

Drakess oversaw Tunngasuaq's training with obsessive precision. The dragon's flight endurance was tested in the vast underground chambers of Mu, forcing him to navigate narrow tunnels at high speeds. Simulated attacks, using weapons scavenged from Human stockpiles, ensured he could withstand gunfire, explosives, and even crude nuclear forces.

"We cannot account for every variable," Drakess warned V-Kar. "The past is a labyrinth of possibilities. Even the smallest deviation could unravel our plans."

V-Kar stood at the edge of the cavern, his golden eyes locked on Tunngasuaq. "He will succeed. Failure is not an option."

V-KAR'S EPIC

The Strategy

The Venomous Elite provided detailed maps of early Human civilizations, focusing on critical choke points in history. Tunngasuaq's mission was clear:

Target Humanity's First Steps!

Tunngasuaq would strike before the rise of organized civilizations, ensuring Humanity remained scattered and unable to progress. Early settlements like Göbekli Tepe and Jericho were identified as prime targets.

The fertile crescent, where Humans first domesticated plants and animals, was to be scorched. Without agriculture, Humans would struggle to form stable societies.

The destruction would be so thorough that no myths, no stories, and no whispers of Human unity would survive.

Tunngasuaq listened in silence as V-Kar outlined the mission. "You will be our vengeance," V-Kar said. "You will ensure that they never rise."

The Lizardfolk's Struggles

While Tunngasuaq prepared for his mission, the rest of the lizardkin faced a harsh reality: Humanity's dominance over the surface was growing, and their hidden strongholds were increasingly vulnerable.

By the 1950s, Human exploration had reached unprecedented levels. Advances in geology, mining, and subterranean mapping brought Humans dangerously close to the lizardkin's hidden sanctuaries.

In Mu, Venomous scouts reported the presence of Human mining operations less than 10 miles from their outer tunnels. In Babylon, archaeologists unearthed fragments of ancient lizardkin structures, their strange carvings sparking whispers of lost civilizations.

Kwekwe addressed the council with growing urgency. "The Humans are becoming too bold," she said. "We cannot rely on myths and shadows alone to keep them at bay."

Sabotage And Subterfuge

The Venomous Elite launched a series of covert operations to slow Human progress.

Explosions were triggered deep within Human mining sites, creating collapses that discouraged further excavation. Survivors told stories of strange noises and glowing eyes, fueling myths of "monsters in the deep."

Venomous agents planted artifacts and symbols near Human excavation sites, reinforcing superstitions about cursed ground and vengeful spirits.

Erasing Evidence

Teams were dispatched to recover or destroy lizardkin artifacts before Humans could study them. In one notable incident, a team infiltrated a museum in Cairo, stealing back an ancient lizardkin tablet that had been mistaken for a piece of early Mesopotamian art.

The Orb's Dormancy

Despite their best efforts, the lizardkin knew their plans could not fully unfold until 2002, when the orb would reawaken and allow them to manipulate the timeline once more.

The orb, now encased in a reinforced chamber beneath Mu, remained a symbol of both hope and dread. V-Kar often visited the chamber, standing silently before the artifact as if willing it to activate.

"We cannot act until it awakens," Wigwas reminded him during one such visit. "The past and the future are locked until then. Until that moment, we must endure."

V-Kar's claws scraped against the stone walls. "Endurance is not enough. We must prepare for every outcome. If the orb fails us, Humanity will be the death of us all."

Humanity's Growing Strength

Above the surface, Humanity continued its relentless march of progress. By the late 21st century, Humans had developed satellites, nuclear weapons, and global communication networks. Their knowledge of the world - and their capacity for destruction - was unparalleled.

V-KAR'S EPIC

The Venomous Elite, still embedded in Human society, struggled to keep pace. Kwekwe, speaking before the council, acknowledged the grim truth.

"They now have eyes in the sky and weapons that can obliterate entire cities," she said. "If we are discovered, we will not survive."

V-Kar, however, remained defiant. "Let them grow. Let them reach their peak. When the time comes, we will strike, and their fall will be all the greater."

The Final Countdown

As the year 2002 approached, the lizardkin's plans began to take shape. Tunngasuaq's preparations were nearly complete, and the orb's dormancy was expected to end soon.

The lizardkin council convened one final time to discuss the implications of their actions.

"If Tunngasuaq succeeds, Humanity will be erased from the timeline," Wigwas said. "But if he fails, Plan B will destroy the timeline entirely. We must ensure there is no failure."

V-Kar stood, his presence commanding. "There will be no failure. The dragon will rise, and the world will burn. Humanity will be forgotten, and the lizardkin will reign eternal."

The council roared in approval, their voices echoing through the underground chambers.

V-KAR'S EPIC

The Final Trial Of Tunngasuaq

In the closing days before 2002, Tunngasuaq completed his final trial: a full simulation of his mission, including navigating through ancient terrain, facing simulated Human defenses, and erasing early settlements.

When the simulation ended, Tunngasuaq stood tall, his eyes burning with determination.

"I am ready," he said, his voice deep and resonant. "Send me back, and I will end them."

Chapter 40: The Dragon and the Luminary

The obsidian orb flared to life, its dormant runes glowing brighter than ever before. The chamber beneath Mu, filled with the lizardkin's most elite council members, trembled as the air grew thick with energy. Tunngasuaq, the dragon of dragons, stood at the center of the chamber, his wings fully extended, his massive form radiating raw power.

The runes on the orb shifted one final time, forming a spiral of light that enveloped Tunngasuaq. In an instant, the dragon was gone, hurled backward through the fabric of time to fulfill his mission - to end Humanity before it began.

A Divine Guardian Awaits

Tunngasuaq emerged into the 2022 skies, his massive wings casting a shadow over the lush, untouched earth below. The air hummed with a primordial energy, thick and alive with the essence of creation. Below him lay the vast and sprawling metropolis.

But he was not alone.

Hovering above the land, a being of radiant light awaited him - a Luminary, its form both Humanoid and infinite, shimmering with a golden brilliance that defied comprehension. Its presence was overwhelming, a manifestation of both timeless wisdom and boundless power.

Tunngasuaq roared, his flames erupting toward the figure in defiance. "You will not stop me, spirit!"

The Luminary raised its hand, and the fire was halted mid-air, dissipating into harmless embers. Its voice, a blend of many tones, echoed through Tunngasuaq's mind:

"You are not the first, nor shall you be the last. The balance of time cannot be broken, even by one such as you."

The Battle Unfolds

The skies darkened as Tunngasuaq and the Luminary clashed, their battle shaking the heavens and the earth.

Tunngasuaq unleashed torrents of fire, his flames scorching the land and skies alike. He lunged with claws sharper than any blade, his roars splitting the air like thunder.

His fire struck mountains, melting them into rivers of molten rock, and his claws tore through ancient forests, leaving scars upon the earth itself.

The Luminary responded with blinding light and celestial energy, its movements graceful yet devastating. With every motion, it created shields of shimmering gold, turning Tunngasuaq's ferocity into harmless wind.

The Luminary wielded the forces of creation itself, hurling bursts of energy that cracked the sky and redirected Tunngasuaq's destruction.

From the earth below, early Humans huddled in awe and terror, their eyes fixed on the battle above. To them, it was a clash of gods - a great serpent of fire and a divine angel of light, battling for the fate of their fragile existence.

The Turning Point

The battle raged for what felt like an eternity, neither side gaining a decisive advantage. Tunngasuaq, though relentless, began to tire. His fire dimmed, and his wings grew heavy from the Luminary's relentless counterattacks.

The Luminary, sensing the shift, raised its hands to the sky. From the heavens descended a sword of pure light, its edges glowing with the power of creation.

"This ends now," the Luminary declared, its voice filled with divine authority.

As the Luminary plunged the sword toward Tunngasuaq, the dragon let out one final roar, a cry of defiance that shook the earth to its core. The sword struck true, piercing the dragon's heart. His massive form convulsed, his fire extinguished.

But as Tunngasuaq fell, his essence scattered into the winds, leaving behind an indelible mark on the earth and its people.

The Luminary spoke to Humanity one final time:

"From chaos, hope is forged. Remember this battle, and let it guide you toward the light."

V-Kar Awakens In A New World

In the year 2007 AD, deep beneath the earth, V-Kar's hibernation chamber cracked open once more. The world he emerged into was not the same one he had left.

The lizardkin's sanctuaries remained hidden, but the surface world had changed beyond recognition. The Humans had advanced far beyond what V-Kar had anticipated:

Quantum Physics: Humanity had unlocked secrets of time and space, though only fragments of this knowledge had reached the general public.

Genetic Engineering: Humans now possessed the ability to manipulate life itself, creating hybrids and curing diseases once thought untouchable.

Space Travel: The stars were no longer out of reach. Humanity had begun exploring their solar system and dreaming of colonizing other worlds.

But most alarming of all was the subtle leakage of knowledge into Human culture. Through movies, novels, and art, Humans were becoming increasingly aware of concepts like hidden civilizations, reptilian overlords, and ancient wars between gods and dragons.

The Rebels' Presence

V-Kar quickly learned that Humanity's advancements had not occurred in isolation. The Luminaries - the same beings who had stopped Tunngasuaq in the ancient past - had subtly guided Humanity's progress, ensuring their survival and growth. These "Rebels," as V-Kar called them, were now deeply embedded in Human society.

Their influence was everywhere:

Cryptic Messages: Hidden in art, literature, and film, subtly encouraging Humans to question their reality and seek the truth.

Technological Leaps: Breakthroughs in physics and engineering that seemed almost too advanced to be Human.

Unified Hope: A growing sense of global unity and resilience, even in the face of division and war.

V-Kar's Struggle

For the first time in his long existence, V-Kar felt truly cornered. The orb, now completely dormant, offered no path backward in time. The center of time had shifted to 2020, and with it, the lizardkin's ability to rewrite history was gone.

He paced the underground council chamber, his golden eyes blazing with frustration.

V-KAR'S EPIC

"We have spent millennia preparing for this moment," he growled. "And yet, they are stronger than ever. We are surrounded by their technology, their armies, their myths. The Humans have become... untouchable."

Wigwas, ever calm, replied, "We still have the orb. It may yet awaken again, and with it, we may find a way forward."

V-Kar clenched his claws. "Forward? No. Forward is where they wait for us. The rebels... these Luminaries... they will not allow us to rise."

The Final War Looms

As the center of time solidified, the lizardkin's secrets became harder to keep. Human myths of angels, demons, and dragons began to merge with modern conspiracies of hidden reptilian overlords. The once-hidden lizardkin empire was now at greater risk of exposure than ever before.

And above it all, the Luminaries continued to guide Humanity, their presence growing stronger as the final confrontation drew near.

V-Kar, standing at the edge of his crumbling empire, gazed into the darkness.

"This is not over," he hissed. "If we cannot destroy them in the past, we will destroy them in the future. Humanity will fall, and we will reclaim this world."

Chapter 41: Plans of the Hegemon and Humanity's Awakening

V-KAR'S EPIC

Deep within the underground stronghold beneath Mu, V-Kar paced the great council chamber. The once-mighty lizardkin empire had been reduced to shadows, their power fragile and fleeting. The orb lay dormant, its runes cold and unresponsive. The timeline had solidified, leaving them with no path backward, and Humanity had grown into a juggernaut - technologically advanced, culturally united in ways that made them more dangerous than ever.

But V-Kar, ever defiant, refused to accept defeat.

"This is not the end," he declared, his voice reverberating through the chamber. "The Humans may think they control this world, but they are blind to their vulnerabilities. If we cannot erase them from the past, we will unmake them in the future."

Plan C: The Final Future
V-Kar outlined his vision to the council, a bold and desperate plan:

The Venomous Elite would infiltrate Human societies, stoking divisions through manipulation of media, politics, and culture. Their goal was to fragment Humanity, turning their strength against them.

"They are strong when they are united," V-Kar said. "We must fracture them before they fracture us."

V-KAR'S EPIC

Advanced Bio-Weapons

The scientists of Mu, led by Drakess's successors, would engineer new biological weapons designed to target Humans exclusively. These weapons would be released subtly, creating pandemics that would weaken Human populations over decades.

With Humanity weakened, the lizardkin would claim the Earth's resources, using their genetic engineering advancements to evolve themselves into beings capable of thriving in any environment.

"We will outlast them," V-Kar concluded. "This world will belong to us once more."

While V-Kar plotted in the shadows, Humanity was beginning to piece together the truth of their ancient adversaries.

The Rebels' Influence

The Luminaries, or "Rebels," who had guided Humanity from the shadows for millennia, intensified their efforts as the center of time approached. Their goal was clear: prepare Humanity for the inevitable confrontation with the lizardkin.

Films, books, and television series about ancient wars, hidden civilizations, and reptilian overlords became increasingly popular. Stories of dragons and angels battling for the soul of Humanity mirrored the events of Tunngasuaq's failed mission.

V-KAR'S EPIC

Subtle messages of unity and resilience were embedded in these narratives, encouraging Humanity to stand together against unseen threats.

Breakthroughs in encryption, quantum physics, and genetic engineering were subtly introduced to Human scientists, ensuring Humanity's advancements kept pace with the lizardkin's secret technologies.

Space travel became a priority, with whispers of colonizing other worlds growing louder among Human leaders.

The Luminaries encouraged global cooperation through environmental crises, space exploration, and shared cultural myths. Slowly, Humanity began to unite under a common purpose, their divisions weakening in the face of existential challenges.

<u>Discoveries In Ancient Texts</u>

In the early 1990s, archaeologists in South America uncovered a cache of ancient Mayan glyphs, hidden deep within a cave. The glyphs told a story of a great serpent and a radiant angel who battled for the fate of Humanity.

The discovery shocked the scientific community. The story closely mirrored biblical texts, particularly the Book of Revelation, and added new details about ancient myths of angels, dragons, and a war for the soul of Humanity.

"The parallels are undeniable," said Dr. Elise Markov, a leading archaeologist. "These texts suggest a shared mythological foundation across cultures, one that predates written history."

Unbeknownst to the researchers, the glyphs had been planted centuries earlier by Venomous agents seeking to manipulate Humanity's myths. But the message backfired - Humans interpreted the story as a rallying cry, a reminder of their resilience against unimaginable odds.

V-Kar's Struggles In A Changing World

As Humanity grew more aware of their hidden history, V-Kar found it increasingly difficult to maintain the secrecy of the lizardkin's existence. The Venomous Elite reported increasing Human activity near their sanctuaries. Drones and satellites, equipped with cutting-edge imaging technology, were uncovering underground anomalies.

In Mu, a scouting party intercepted a Human drone just miles from the entrance to their stronghold. The footage it captured had already been transmitted to the surface.

"This cannot continue," Wigwas said during a council meeting. "The Humans are too close. If they discover us, we will have no way to defend ourselves."

V-Kar slammed his clawed hand against the table. "Then we will eliminate the threat before it spreads."

The Rebels' Interference

As if the Humans weren't enough, the Luminaries began to intervene directly. Their presence became more pronounced, appearing in strange lights over Human cities, in whispered messages during Human dreams, and even in unexplained technological malfunctions.

V-KAR'S EPIC

During a mission to sabotage a Human research facility, a Venomous agent reported encountering a Luminary.

"It spoke without words," the agent said, trembling. "It told me to stop, that my actions would only hasten our end."

The encounter rattled the council. Kwekwe, ever skeptical, dismissed the report as Human trickery, but Wigwas was less certain.

"They are watching us," she said quietly. "And they are warning us."

The Center Of Time Approaches

As time neared its new focal point in 2020, the tension between the lizardkin, the Humans, and the Luminaries reached a breaking point.

V-Kar, now facing the greatest challenge of his reign, stood alone in the chamber where the orb had once pulsed with life. Its runes remained dormant, refusing to grant him the power he so desperately needed.

"We are running out of time," he murmured to himself. "But time is all we have left."

The orb, silent and still, seemed to mock him.

The Final Confrontation Looms

Above the surface, Humanity unknowingly prepared for the battle to come. The Luminaries continued their subtle guidance, ensuring that Humans would face the coming storm with hope and strength.

Below, V-Kar and his council worked tirelessly to finalize their plans. The lizardkin's very survival depended on their ability to outmaneuver both Humanity and the rebels.

As the clock ticked toward 2020, the world held its breath. The battle for the future of Earth was about to begin.

<u>Chapter 42: The Final Preparations</u>

Deep beneath the earth, in the sanctuaries of Mu, Babylon, and Atlantis's submerged ruins, the lizardkin prepared for their greatest and possibly final battle. The center of time was solidifying in 2020 AD, and with it came the growing presence of the Luminaries and Humanity's accelerating awareness of their ancient adversaries.

V-Kar stood at the head of his council, his golden eyes burning with determination. Though the orb remained dormant, he knew that their survival depended on decisive action.

"We must strike before they unite," he growled. "The Humans are weak individually, but with the rebels guiding them, they will become unstoppable."

<u>The Venomous Elite's Strategy</u>

Kwekwe outlined a plan of infiltration and sabotage, targeting Humanity's key infrastructure:

Venomous agents would disrupt satellite networks, spreading misinformation and panic. The goal was to isolate Humanity's factions, making coordinated resistance impossible.

"Their strength lies in their connectivity," Kwekwe explained. "We will cut the threads that bind them."

Underground teams would target power grids and fuel supplies, creating widespread blackouts.

"Let them stumble in the dark," she said. "While they falter, we will rise."

Scientists in Mu accelerated their bioengineering projects, creating enhanced lizardkin soldiers and experimenting with diseases designed to target Humans.

Wigwas, however, voiced her concerns. "This will weaken them, yes, but it will not be enough. The rebels' influence is stronger than we anticipated."

The Berserkers' Readiness

The remaining Berserkers, though few, trained relentlessly in the vast subterranean caverns. These dragon-blooded warriors were the lizardkin's last line of offense, their strength unmatched by anything Humanity could produce.

Tunngasuaq's loss still weighed heavily on their kind, but his name became a rallying cry among the Berserkers. They sought to avenge their fallen kin by unleashing their fury on the surface world.

Above the surface, Humanity's awakening was reaching a critical point. The Luminaries, guiding Humanity with subtle precision, had begun to foster cooperation between governments, scientific communities, and ordinary citizens.

Appearing more frequently as streaks of light in the sky, whispers in dreams, and sudden bursts of inspiration, the Luminaries worked to prepare Humanity for the coming conflict.

V-KAR'S EPIC

Innovations in quantum physics, encryption, and genetic engineering accelerated. The Luminaries guided scientists toward breakthroughs that seemed almost miraculous, giving Humanity tools to rival even the lizardkin's advanced systems.

The Luminaries encouraged the spread of stories and myths that emphasized unity and resilience.

Films, books, and games about Humanity overcoming ancient threats became wildly popular, subtly preparing the population for the truth of their shared history.

Secret collaborations between nations created a network of orbital defenses, underground bunkers, and experimental weaponry. Though officially unexplained, these measures were designed with knowledge provided by the Luminaries.

The Revelation Movement

Among the general public, a growing movement began to piece together fragments of suppressed truths. Known as the Revelation Movement, this group connected myths of angels, demons, dragons, and ancient wars with modern conspiracies about hidden reptilian overlords.

Leaders of the movement spoke of a coming reckoning, citing ancient texts and unexplained phenomena as evidence. Though dismissed by mainstream media, the movement gained traction, fueled by leaked documents and whistleblowers claiming to have encountered lizardkin technology.

"The stories are all connected," said Elise Markov, an archaeologist turned Revelation leader. "Dragons, angels, serpents - they're not myths. They're memories of a war older than history itself."

V-Kar Faces New Challenges

In the depths of Mu, V-Kar felt the weight of the shifting timeline pressing upon him. The Humans' rapid advancements and the Luminaries' growing influence left little room for error.

During a private meeting with Wigwas, he voiced his frustration. "They are stronger than we imagined. Every plan we make, they counter before it even begins."

Wigwas nodded solemnly. "The rebels are guiding them. They see what we cannot."

"What of the orb?" V-Kar demanded. "It must awaken soon."

Wigwas hesitated. "We believe it will activate when the center of time fully stabilizes. But there is no guarantee it will respond to us."

The Struggle To Remain Hidden

Human exploration of subterranean regions had intensified, with drones and seismic imaging bringing them perilously close to the lizardkin's sanctuaries.

One Venomous scout reported a near-disaster when a Human research team stumbled upon an ancient lizardkin glyph in the Amazon basin. Though the site was sabotaged before the Humans could learn its significance, the incident underscored the growing danger of exposure.

"We cannot remain hidden much longer," Kwekwe warned the council. "The Humans are closing in, and their technology sees through stone."

The Luminaries Make Contact

In the skies above North America, a group of Luminaries appeared in their most direct manifestation yet - blazing streaks of light that converged over a remote mountain range. Witnesses described a feeling of overwhelming peace and clarity, as if the very presence of the Luminaries had calmed their minds.

This event, dubbed the Aurora Contact, became a flashpoint in Human history. World leaders, facing pressure from the Revelation Movement and their own secret knowledge, began to acknowledge the possibility of non-Human influence on Earth's history.

Though no official statements were made, whispers spread among the populace: Humanity was not alone, and their allies were watching.

The Final Countdown

As the year 2020 drew closer, both sides prepared for the inevitable confrontation:

V-KAR'S EPIC

V-Kar ordered the final activation of their genetic superweapons and the Berserkers' mobilization. Hidden launch sites for seismic destabilization weapons were prepared deep beneath Mu and Babylon.

Humanity

Guided by the Luminaries, Humanity strengthened their global defense systems, creating countermeasures for subterranean attacks and preparing for possible invasions from below.

In the closing days of 2011, the obsidian orb began to hum faintly, its runes flickering for the first time in decades.

V-Kar, standing alone in the chamber, placed his claws upon its surface. "The time has come," he whispered.

But as the runes began to align, the orb's light suddenly flared, and a voice filled the chamber - a voice that was not his own.

"The center of time solidifies. The reckoning begins. Prepare yourselves for the end of all things."

Chapter 43: The Voice Of The Orb

The obsidian orb pulsed violently, its runes shifting in chaotic patterns as light filled the chamber deep beneath Mu. V-Kar stood alone, his massive frame bathed in the eerie glow. The hum of the orb resonated through the stone walls, a sound that was not just heard but felt - deep within his bones, as if the artifact were reaching into his very essence.

For decades, the orb had been silent, its purpose unclear as Humanity advanced and the lizardkin dwindled in secrecy. Now, that it was near the center of time in 2012, it had reawakened - but its energy was unlike anything V-Kar had experienced before.

The runes on its surface began to align, forming intricate spirals and glyphs that radiated impossible clarity. Then, the hum shifted, turning into a voice that filled the chamber - a voice layered with tones, at once both calm and commanding, alien yet unmistakably ancient.

The Voice Speaks

"You have touched the edge of time and been found wanting."

The voice echoed, its weight pressing down on V-Kar. He instinctively braced himself, his claws curling into the stone floor.

"You have sought dominion over the cycle, but the cycle does not bend. You are not its master. You are its fragment."

"What are you?" V-Kar growled, his voice defiant despite the overwhelming presence. "What do you want of me?"

The orb's glow intensified, the runes shifting to form a pattern that resembled an unbroken chain.

"We are the architects of the loom, the weavers of the thread. You are but a single strand, stretched too thin."

V-Kar's eyes narrowed. "You speak in riddles. If you are so powerful, why do you hide behind words?"

The voice did not waver.

"You misunderstand. We are not hidden. We are the balance. You have disrupted the balance, and now you will listen."

The Warning

The orb's runes began to project images - visions of worlds collapsing into themselves, stars burning out, and civilizations erased from history.

"The cycle is fragile. You have sought to alter its center, to rewrite its foundation. This is not allowed."

V-Kar snarled, his tail lashing against the chamber wall. "Not allowed? This world was ours long before the Humans crawled from the dirt. We will take it back!"

The voice grew sharper, more deliberate.

"Your claim to this world is as fleeting as theirs. The cycle does not belong to you. It belongs to all."

V-KAR'S EPIC

"Empty words," V-Kar spat. "You are no god. If you were, you would have struck me down already."

The orb pulsed again, the chamber shaking with its intensity.

"We are not gods. We are the loom. And the loom does not strike - it weaves. Your thread is frayed, but it has not yet snapped. Listen carefully, for this is your only warning."

The Threat

The images projected by the orb shifted again, showing the lizardkin's hidden sanctuaries collapsing under seismic tremors, their Berserkers overwhelmed by Human forces armed with weapons far beyond their comprehension.

"You have seen the Humans rise, guided by those who defy entropy. They are protected because they understand the loom. Their resilience is not chance - it is purpose. They are the thread you cannot sever."

V-Kar's golden eyes blazed with fury. "Then we will unravel the loom itself if we must!"

The voice paused, the silence more oppressive than the words.

"Unravel the loom, and you unravel yourself. You are not above the cycle, V-Kar. You are within it. Should you persist in your defiance, you will be unmade - not by us, but by your own hand."

The Choice

The runes on the orb began to stabilize, forming a single glowing spiral at its center. The voice softened, its tone shifting to one of finality.

"You have a choice, Hegemon. Persist, and the center of time will collapse. The threads of history will dissolve, and neither you nor the Humans will remain. Or relent, and accept your place within the loom. Let the threads weave as they must, and the cycle will endure."

V-Kar stood frozen, the weight of the words pressing down on him. He was silent for a long moment, his claws tightening around the edge of the pedestal where the orb rested.

"If I relent," he said finally, his voice low, "what happens to my kind?"

The orb glowed faintly, its light pulsing like a heartbeat.

"You will endure, as you have always endured. The Humans will rise, and you will adapt. The loom will weave a future where all threads are given their place. But this future cannot be forced - it must be earned."

A Reluctant Decision

V-Kar let out a slow, rumbling breath. He hated the idea of surrendering to forces he could not control, hated the thought of ceding any ground to the Humans or the Luminaries. But the visions the orb had shown him - the destruction of both his people and the world itself - were not something he could ignore.

He stepped back from the orb, his golden eyes narrowing. "If what you say is true, then I will wait. But know this: if the Humans overstep, if they seek to erase us as we sought to erase them, I will fight with everything I have."

The voice responded, its tone resolute.

"That is the loom's decision to make, not yours. Remember this moment, V-Kar. You have been given the chance to endure. Do not squander it."

With that, the orb's light dimmed, and the runes fell still. The chamber returned to silence, but V-Kar remained standing, his mind racing with thoughts of the future.

The Weight Of The Loom

As he left the chamber, V-Kar felt the burden of the orb's warning settle upon him. The lizardkin's survival depended on restraint, on adaptation - a path he had never been inclined to follow.

In the shadows of Mu, his council awaited his orders. Kwekwe stepped forward, her voice filled with urgency. "What did it say?"

V-Kar's gaze swept over the council, his expression unreadable. "It said we must wait. But waiting does not mean surrender. Prepare our forces. Watch the Humans. If they falter, we will not hesitate to act."

The council nodded, but Wigwas stepped closer, her voice low. "And if the orb is right? If the cycle cannot be broken?"

V-Kar's eyes burned with defiance. "Then we will find another way. The loom may weave, but I will not be its puppet."

V-KAR'S EPIC

Chapter 44: Threads Of Defiance And Unity

The obsidian orb's warning weighed heavily on V-Kar as he returned to his council chambers deep beneath Mu. The once-proud Hegemon, who had spent centuries trying to bend the timeline to his will, now faced the grim reality of his limitations. The cycle would not bow to him; his choices were stark: adapt or be unmade.

But adaptation, for V-Kar, was not surrender - it was strategy.

As V-Kar explained the orb's message, the council erupted into heated debate.

Kwekwe, ever the pragmatist, scoffed at the notion of waiting. "The orb speaks in riddles," she hissed. "Its warnings are meant to scare us into inaction. If we wait, the Humans will grow stronger, and we will be finished."

Wigwas, on the other hand, advocated caution. "The orb has proven its power," she said. "It showed us the truth of the Architects and the Luminaries. If we defy it, we risk everything - not just our people, but the world itself."

V-Kar silenced them with a single motion of his claw. "We will wait," he said, his voice cold and deliberate. "But waiting does not mean idleness. We will prepare for every possibility, and we will ensure that the Humans do not surpass us unchecked."

V-KAR'S EPIC

Rebuilding In Secrecy

Under V-Kar's orders, the lizardkin began fortifying their subterranean sanctuaries. In Mu, the scientists ramped up their bioengineering projects, creating enhanced lizardkin capable of surviving on the surface if needed.

The Berserkers trained relentlessly, their numbers bolstered by new hybrid experiments. Though few, they were stronger and faster than ever before, ready to be unleashed should the need arise.

The Venomous Elite continued their infiltration of Human society, working to manipulate the flow of information and sow seeds of division.

"We cannot attack," V-Kar told the council, "but we can weaken them from within. Let the Humans fight each other. Let them grow suspicious of the rebels' guidance. The more divided they are, the stronger we will become."

The Hegemon's Secret Plan

Privately, V-Kar began working on a contingency - one he shared with no one, not even Wigwas. Deep in the archives of Mu, he studied the ancient texts left behind by Kaelyss, piecing together fragments of the lizardkin's earliest history.

He theorized that there might be a way to break the cycle without unraveling it - a hidden thread within the loom that could be pulled to reshape the weave. If he could find it, he believed he could tip the balance in his favor without invoking the orb's catastrophic warnings.

"It is not rebellion," he murmured to himself as he traced the glowing glyphs in the texts. "It is… refinement."

Above the surface, Humanity was on the cusp of a new era. The Luminaries, now working more openly than ever, continued to guide Humanity toward unity and strength, preparing them for the conflict they knew was inevitable.

The Age Of Discovery

By 2015, Humanity's scientific advancements had reached a tipping point. Under the subtle influence of the Luminaries, breakthroughs in quantum mechanics, genetic engineering, and AI technology accelerated.

Scientists developed a global quantum communication network, allowing for instantaneous, unhackable information exchange. This innovation ensured that Humanity's leaders could coordinate without fear of interference.

Unknown to them, the Luminaries had subtly provided key insights to make this possible.

Advances in genetic engineering eradicated diseases, extended lifespans, and even allowed for the creation of hybrid organisms designed for specific tasks.

This technology, though celebrated, also raised ethical concerns. Luminary influence ensured it was used responsibly, preventing the kind of weaponization the lizardkin had perfected.

Humanity's reach expanded beyond Earth. Colonization of the Moon and Mars became a reality, with plans for deep-space exploration already underway.

The Luminaries encouraged this outward focus, knowing that Humanity's unity would be strengthened by the shared goal of reaching the stars.

Reinterpreting Myths

Stories of dragons, angels, and demons were revisited, presented as allegories for the struggle between chaos and order, fear and hope.

Films and novels portrayed the "monsters" of old as misunderstood beings, fostering empathy and curiosity rather than fear.

The Revelation Movement's Growth

The Revelation Movement, once dismissed as fringe conspiracy theorists, gained mainstream attention. Their claims of hidden reptilian civilizations and ancient wars were bolstered by newly uncovered artifacts and texts.

Though unaware of the Luminaries' role, the movement unknowingly aligned with their goal of preparing Humanity for the truth.

V-KAR'S EPIC

Direct Luminary Contact

In 2017, a global phenomenon occurred. Across the world, people reported vivid dreams of glowing figures speaking in soothing tones, urging them to "prepare for the dawn."

These dreams, later dubbed the Aurora Visions, sparked a worldwide shift in consciousness. Religious leaders, scientists, and politicians alike began speaking of a coming change - one that would require Humanity to unite like never before.

Though the Luminaries had carefully orchestrated the event, they ensured their presence remained ambiguous. To most, they were seen as divine messengers or benevolent extraterrestrials, their true nature still shrouded in mystery.

The Loom Tightens

As the center of time solidified, the threads of the past, present, and future grew taut. Both Humanity and the lizardkin stood on the brink, their fates intertwined in ways neither fully understood.

V-Kar, though outwardly resolute, felt the strain of the orb's warning with every passing day. The Luminaries' influence was growing, and Humanity's strength was becoming undeniable.

But in his mind, the secret plan took shape - a plan to reshape the cycle without breaking it, to weave a future where the lizardkin could reclaim their place without triggering the orb's catastrophic consequences.

Above the surface, Humanity prepared for the unknown, their unity growing stronger under the Luminaries' watchful guidance.

And in the shadows, the final threads were pulled tighter, the loom preparing to weave the climactic pattern of the cycle.

Chapter 45: Hidden Plans And Unveiled Truths

Deep beneath Mu, V-Kar retreated to a secluded chamber known only to him. The walls, etched with runes from the lizardkin's earliest history, glowed faintly in the dim light. Before him lay the fragments of knowledge left by Kaelyss and the obsidian orb, alongside countless scrolls and tablets unearthed over millennia.

The orb's warning had forced his hand: outright defiance of the cycle would lead to ruin. But V-Kar believed there was a third way - an opportunity buried in the texts of their past.

A Forgotten Thread

V-Kar poured over the glyphs and runes, tracing patterns that hinted at a deeper truth about the cycle. One recurring phrase caught his attention:

"The unseen thread binds what the loom rejects."

It was a cryptic reference, but V-Kar interpreted it as a potential loophole - a thread of the cycle hidden within the weave, one that could be pulled without unmaking the whole.

His theory was simple yet audacious: if he could find this unseen thread, he could subtly alter the loom without defying its rules. The lizardkin would not need to destroy Humanity; instead, they could reshape the timeline to ensure their survival alongside them - or, more ambitiously, above them.

V-KAR'S EPIC

The Key To The Thread
V-Kar believed the key to this thread lay within the orb itself. Though dormant, the orb's sporadic energy fluctuations suggested it still responded to certain stimuli. He hypothesized that the orb's runes, when aligned with the proper frequencies, could reveal the thread's location.

"It is not rebellion," V-Kar muttered, his claws scratching across the stone table. "It is... refinement."

But testing this theory required immense precision - and secrecy. V-Kar knew that even his closest allies, like Wigwas, might question the risks involved. For now, he worked alone, hiding his efforts from both the council and the Humans.

The Revelation Movement Gains Ground
Above the surface, Humanity was inching closer to uncovering the lizardkin's existence. The Revelation Movement, bolstered by new discoveries and growing public interest, was on the verge of a breakthrough.

In early 2010, a team of Revelation archaeologists, led by Dr. Elise Markov, uncovered a hidden cache of ancient texts beneath the Andes Mountains. Among the artifacts was a tablet inscribed with glyphs identical to those found in the ruins of Babylon and Mu - glyphs unmistakably reptilian in origin.

The tablet depicted a battle between two forces: a great serpent, wreathed in fire, and a figure of radiant light. The imagery was strikingly similar to the myths of dragons and angels found in cultures across the globe.

"It's all connected," Markov said during a press conference. "These glyphs are proof that these myths are not just stories - they're fragments of a shared history."

The Movement's Growing Influence

The Revelation Movement's discoveries resonated with a global audience. Through social media, documentaries, and viral campaigns, they spread their message: Humanity was not alone, and their history was far older than anyone had imagined.

Stories of hidden civilizations and ancient wars began to dominate public discourse. Though many dismissed the movement as conspiracy theorists, their evidence was compelling enough to spark widespread curiosity.

Governments around the world began to monitor the movement closely, concerned about the potential implications of their discoveries. Classified documents about unexplained phenomena and hidden sites were leaked, further fueling the movement's momentum.

The Luminaries subtly encouraged the movement, ensuring that Humanity's growing awareness remained focused on unity and resilience rather than fear. Their influence was felt in the Movement's messaging, which emphasized cooperation and hope.

V-KAR'S EPIC

A Growing Threat To Secrecy

The lizardkin, watching from the shadows, grew increasingly alarmed by the Revelation Movement's progress. Reports of Human activity near their sanctuaries became more frequent, and Venomous agents struggled to keep up with

sabotaging excavation sites and discrediting evidence.

During a council meeting, Wigwas voiced her concern. "The Humans are piecing together too much. If they uncover one of our sanctuaries, our existence will no longer be a secret."

Kwekwe hissed in frustration. "Let them come. They are no match for us underground."

But V-Kar, his mind still consumed by his secret plan, raised a claw. "No," he said. "If they discover us before we are ready, it will not be a battle - it will be an extermination. We must act carefully."

An Unexpected Encounter

One of the Revelation Movement's expeditions came perilously close to the underground sanctuary near Babylon. The Venomous Elite sent a small team to monitor their progress and ensure they found nothing of significance.

But as the team approached, they encountered something unexpected: a Luminary, its form glowing faintly in the darkness, standing between the Humans and the lizardkin's hidden entrance.

The Humans, oblivious to the Luminary's true nature, interpreted its appearance as a divine sign. They recorded the event, describing it as an angel guarding ancient secrets.

The Venomous agents, however, knew better.

"They are protecting the Humans," one agent reported to the council. "They know we're here, and they are shielding them from us."

As the center of time approached, both sides intensified their preparations.

The Lizardfolk: V-Kar's secret plan moved forward in silence, while the council focused on maintaining their secrecy and sabotaging Humanity's progress.

The Humans: Guided by the Luminaries, the Revelation Movement continued to uncover fragments of the lizardkin's history, slowly unraveling the truth.

In the shadows, the orb began to hum faintly once more, its energy stirring as the final threads of the loom aligned.

V-KAR'S EPIC

Chapter 46: The Fall Of Babylon And Atlantis

Beneath the surface of the earth, the lizardkin's relentless mining operations reached critical thresholds. In Babylon and Atlantis, massive caverns had been carved out over centuries, their walls reinforced by advanced lizardkin engineering. The mining served two purposes: extracting rare minerals to power their technology and expanding their sanctuaries in preparation for a growing population and inevitable conflict with Humanity.

But in their haste to secure their future, they had ignored the warnings of seismic instability. Deep beneath these ancient cities, fault lines crisscrossed like veins, and the weight of centuries of excavation had pushed the earth to its breaking point.

Babylon's Collapse

In Babylon, a Venomous scouting party returned with dire news. The largest cavern beneath the city - the Cradle of the Hegemon - had begun to show signs of structural failure. Cracks spread through its walls like spiderwebs, and faint tremors could be felt even in the uppermost tunnels.

"We must halt the mining operations," warned Drakess's successor, an elder scientist named Klyros. "The earth cannot support the strain. If we continue, the entire structure will collapse."

But Kwekwe, overseeing the mining effort, dismissed the concerns. "We are too close to our goal," she hissed. "The

Page 249

Humans will not wait for us to be cautious. We must extract what we need before they discover us."

Klyros appealed to V-Kar, but the Hegemon's response was calculated. "The risk is acceptable," he said. "If Babylon falls, we will retreat to Mu and Atlantis. Our priority is ensuring our survival, not protecting the surface."

The mining continued, and within days, the tremors intensified.

The Collapse

It began with a thunderous roar that echoed through the subterranean chambers. The cracks in the Cradle of the Hegemon widened, and entire sections of the cavern began to cave in. Above ground, the city of Babylon trembled as buildings swayed and collapsed into sinkholes that appeared seemingly out of nowhere.

The Humans of Babylon, unaware of the lizardkin's underground activities, believed they were witnessing divine wrath. They fled in terror as the city crumbled around them, leaving only ruins where a thriving civilization had once stood.

Kwekwe barely escaped the collapse, leading a small group of Venomous Elite through crumbling tunnels to a hidden exit. Klyros, however, was not so fortunate. The elder scientist was last seen attempting to stabilize one of the cavern's support pillars, his fate sealed as the ceiling gave way.

V-KAR'S EPIC

The Surface Perspective

To the Humans, Babylon's destruction was a cataclysmic event beyond their understanding. They recorded it in their myths as a punishment from the gods - a tale of hubris and divine retribution that would echo through history.

The lizardkin, watching from the shadows, saw it differently. Babylon had been a vital stronghold, and its loss was a devastating blow to their plans. V-Kar, though outwardly composed, seethed with frustration at the setback.

The Sinking Of Atlantis

In Atlantis, the lizardkin's most ambitious mining operation had unearthed vast reserves of a rare crystalline mineral known as Aetherium, which was critical to powering their advanced technology. The crystals emitted a faint, otherworldly glow, and their energy potential was unmatched by any other resource.

But Aetherium's extraction was perilous. Its removal destabilized the bedrock beneath Atlantis, creating a network of fractures that extended to the ocean floor.

Warnings Ignored

As in Babylon, lizardkin scientists in Atlantis raised alarms about the dangers of continued mining. The ocean itself seemed to protest, with underwater tremors sending shockwaves through the surrounding seabed.

V-KAR'S EPIC

"The caverns will flood if we continue," warned Thryka, one of Atlantis's chief engineers. "If the ocean breaches the tunnels, it will take the entire city with it."

But the council in Atlantis, emboldened by their success in extracting Aetherium, refused to halt operations. "The Humans are spreading across the surface," argued one councilor. "If we stop now, we risk losing our technological advantage."

V-Kar, who had relocated to Atlantis after Babylon's collapse, reluctantly approved the continued mining. "If Atlantis falls," he said coldly, "then let it fall. But we will ensure that our knowledge and resources survive."

The Breach

The end came swiftly and without warning. During a routine extraction, a critical support structure failed, causing a massive cave-in. The tremor triggered a chain reaction, collapsing the tunnels closest to the seabed. Water began to pour into the caverns with unstoppable force.

Within hours, the entire network was flooded, and the weight of the ocean caused Atlantis itself to sink. Towers that had once reached for the sky disappeared beneath the waves, their lights extinguished forever.

The lizardkin who managed to escape fled to Mu, their last remaining stronghold. Those who remained in Atlantis either drowned or were crushed as the city was swallowed by the sea.

Human Myths

To the Humans, the sinking of Atlantis became a legend - a tale of a great and advanced civilization lost to the depths. Stories of its splendor and mysterious disappearance would captivate Humanity for millennia, inspiring countless expeditions and theories.

For the lizardkin, however, it was a bitter reminder of their fallibility. Atlantis had been their greatest achievement, and its loss marked the end of their dominance on the surface.

In the wake of these disasters, the lizardkin retreated further into secrecy. Mu, hidden deep beneath the earth and far from Human exploration, became their final refuge. The losses of Babylon and Atlantis weighed heavily on V-Kar, but he refused to show weakness.

"Our mistakes have cost us," he said during a council meeting. "But they have also taught us. From now on, we will act with precision and caution. The Humans cannot discover us - not yet."

Wigwas, ever pragmatic, nodded. "The orb remains silent, but its warning still holds. We cannot afford another failure."

A World Forever Changed

Above the surface, the fall of Babylon and Atlantis would leave a profound impact on Human history. These events, interpreted as acts of divine intervention or cosmic justice, become part of Humanity's collective mythology. They serve as warnings against hubris and the fragility of great civilizations.

Below, the lizardkin regrouped, their numbers diminished but their resolve unbroken. V-Kar, though chastened by the orb's warnings and the disasters that followed, continued to plot, his eyes set on the future.

"The cycle has not ended," he told himself. "And I am still its strongest thread."

Chapter 47: Rebuilding In Shadows, Unearthing The Past

Deep beneath the earth in the labyrinthine sanctuary of Mu, the last stronghold of the lizardkin empire, V-Kar gathered his council. The losses of Babylon and Atlantis were profound, but V-Kar refused to let despair take root among his people.

"The Humans may think their gods have protected them," V-Kar declared to the assembly, his golden eyes blazing. "But we are not defeated. The loom continues to weave, and our thread remains unbroken. We will rebuild, stronger and smarter than before."

Refocusing Efforts

The first step was consolidation. V-Kar ordered all remaining resources, artifacts, and surviving lizardkin from Babylon and Atlantis to be brought to Mu. Scientists, engineers, and warriors worked tirelessly to recover what they could from the ruins of their lost cities.

Aetherium Salvage: Teams of Venomous Elite ventured into the flooded depths of Atlantis, using bioengineered diving suits to recover fragments of the precious crystalline material. Though most of it was lost, the small quantities retrieved were stored for critical future projects.

Knowledge Preservation: Ancient tablets and glyphs, many of them damaged during the collapses, were meticulously restored and copied. The lizardkin could not afford to lose the wisdom of their ancestors.

Population Recovery: Genetic engineers began creating hybridized offspring, enhancing their resilience and intelligence. These new generations would be the backbone of their renewed strength.

V-Kar shifted the lizardkin's focus from direct conflict to stealth and subterfuge. Their operations would now prioritize long-term survival over immediate domination.

Mu's tunnels were extended even deeper into the earth, creating a network so vast and hidden that no Human technology could detect it.

Entire biomes were created underground, allowing the lizardkin to farm resources without needing to surface.

The Venomous Elite infiltrated Human governments and academic institutions, spreading misinformation about Atlantis and Babylon to keep Humanity from uncovering the truth.

Myths were distorted, and archaeological evidence was tampered with to ensure that any Human discoveries would lead them astray.

In secret, V-Kar began developing a plan to weaponize the recovered Aetherium. Though its potential was not fully understood, he believed it could be the key to reclaiming dominance when the time was right.

V-KAR'S EPIC

Humanity's Growing Knowledge

On the surface, the collapses of Babylon and Atlantis became the foundation of enduring myths, but the truth behind these events was gradually coming to light.

The Revelation Movement, emboldened by recent archaeological finds, continued to piece together fragments of the past. The discovery of the Babylonian Sinkholes and the Atlantis Ruins provided them with new evidence that ancient civilizations had been far more advanced than previously believed.

Archaeologists uncovered deep tunnels beneath Babylon, filled with strange carvings and artifacts that hinted at non-Human craftsmanship. Though most of the tunnels had collapsed, what remained suggested a sophisticated underground network.

Divers exploring the ocean floor near the supposed location of Atlantis discovered crystalline fragments emitting faint energy signatures. Though dismissed as natural formations by mainstream scientists, members of the Revelation Movement believed they were remnants of a lost technology.

Dr. Elise Markov, a leading figure in the movement, published a groundbreaking theory:

"Babylon and Atlantis were connected by an underground network built by a civilization far older than Humanity. These events were not natural disasters - they were the result of something far more deliberate."

V-KAR'S EPIC

Markov's claims were met with skepticism from traditional scholars, who argued that the evidence was circumstantial at best. But leaked documents from government agencies revealed classified reports about unexplained seismic activity and unnatural structures beneath the ruins.

Public interest surged, and the Revelation Movement gained millions of followers. To many, the idea of a hidden, ancient civilization was no longer fringe speculation - it was a tantalizing possibility.

The Luminaries, watching from the edges of Human awareness, subtly guided the movement to ensure it remained focused on unity and discovery rather than fear and division.

Encouraging Exploration

Luminary-inspired dreams and visions drove scientists and explorers to dig deeper, uncovering clues that aligned with the movement's theories.

Subtle interventions prevented disastrous encounters, ensuring Humanity's progress did not trigger direct conflict with the lizardkin.

The Luminaries used their influence to shape public perception of Atlantis and Babylon. Instead of symbols of destruction, these cities were framed as cautionary tales about the dangers of greed and hubris.

The Loom Tightens

Both sides - the lizardkin in their subterranean sanctuaries and Humanity on the surface - felt the weight of the approaching center of time.

In Mu, V-Kar's scientists detected unusual energy fluctuations emanating from the earth itself. These anomalies, which they believed were tied to the center of time, caused concern among the council.

"These readings suggest instability," Wigwas reported. "If the orb reawakens and we are unprepared, it could bring disaster."

But V-Kar dismissed her warnings. "We will be ready. The Humans are distracted by their myths and false gods. We have time to rebuild and strike when they least expect it."

A World In Flux

Above, Humanity stood on the brink of a new era. The Revelation Movement's discoveries were reshaping public consciousness, and the Luminaries' influence was pushing Humanity toward unprecedented unity and technological advancement.

Below, the lizardkin toiled in secret, their ambitions undiminished despite their losses. For V-Kar, the future remained a battlefield - one where his people would either rise again or vanish into the annals of history.

And in the shadows of the loom, the threads of time pulled tighter, the orb's faint hum growing stronger as the moment of reckoning approached.

Chapter 48: Clashing Shadows And Unearthed Secrets

Deep within Mu, the hum of the orb had grown faintly louder, a constant reminder that the center of time was fast approaching. V-Kar stood at the edge of his council chamber, claws tapping on the stone table as his mind churned with thoughts of the future.

"We are running out of time," Wigwas said, breaking the silence. "The Revelation Movement has uncovered too much. The Humans are no longer stumbling - they are searching."

"They search for ghosts," Kwekwe snapped. "They have yet to find us, and they won't. We've buried ourselves too deeply."

V-Kar silenced them both with a single motion of his claw. "The Humans are dangerous not because of what they know," he growled, "but because of what they will do with it. Their myths have become their truths. They are preparing for war, even if they don't know who their enemy is yet."

The Venomous Elite's Efforts

In response to the Revelation Movement's growing discoveries, the Venomous Elite redoubled their efforts to suppress Human knowledge.

Agents within academic circles discredited key figures of the Revelation Movement, planting false evidence to create divisions and sow doubt.

Texts and artifacts that hinted at the lizardkin's existence were stolen or destroyed before they could be studied.

Sabotage Of Key Expeditions

A critical dig site in the Andes, led by Dr. Elise Markov, was sabotaged. Explosives planted by Venomous agents triggered a controlled collapse, burying the most sensitive discoveries.

Markov survived but was injured, and rumors spread that the incident was no accident.

Despite these efforts, the movement persisted, their resolve only strengthened by the challenges they faced.

Humanity's Unearthed Secrets

Above the surface, the Revelation Movement continued to connect ancient myths with tangible evidence, drawing closer to the truth of the lizardkin's hidden civilization.

Following the collapse in the Andes, Markov's team uncovered a previously hidden chamber near the site. Inside, they found a series of glyphs and carvings depicting a story long forgotten:

The Dryas flood: The carvings showed a wave destroying thewhole earth, with figures resembling Humanoid reptiles fleeing into the depths.

The War of the Serpent and the Light: A serpent wreathed in fire fought against a figure of radiant light, their battle depicted as shaping the world itself.

The Loom of Time: A spiral pattern, similar to the glyphs found in Babylon, hinted at a connection between the serpent, the light, and the very fabric of reality.

Markov's interpretation was clear: "These aren't just myths - they're fragments of history. The serpent represents an ancient civilization, one that existed long before Humanity. And the light… perhaps they weren't gods, but something else entirely."

The Revelation Movement's findings sent shockwaves through the global community.

The Movement Gains Momentum

Markov's discoveries, coupled with leaked government files, fueled widespread belief in the existence of an ancient reptilian civilization.

Documentaries, news reports, and viral campaigns spread the message: Humanity's history was far older and more complex than previously believed.

Governments scrambled to control the narrative, but the truth was slipping through their fingers.

Religious leaders and skeptics clashed over the implications of these findings, while conspiracy theories about hidden reptilian overlords reached a fever pitch.

The Revelation Movement's growing influence brought them perilously close to Mu itself. A major expedition, armed with cutting-edge technology and funded by private backers, set its sights on the Middle East. Their goal was to explore unexplained seismic activity beneath the desert - activity caused by the collapse of Babylon centuries earlier.

V-Kar, aware of the danger, dispatched a team of Venomous Elite to intercept the expedition. Their mission was clear: destroy the Humans' equipment and ensure they uncovered nothing.

The agents sabotaged the expedition's vehicles and planted traps along the desert paths. But as the Humans pressed on, guided by the Luminaries' subtle influence, the Venomous agents found themselves facing unexpected resistance.

A Luminary Intervention

One night, as the agents prepared to strike, the desert was illuminated by a glowing figure descending from the sky. A Luminary, its form shimmering with radiant energy, stood between the Humans and the Venomous agents.

The agents froze, their weapons trembling in their claws. The Luminary spoke without words, its voice resonating directly in their minds:

"Your actions will not change the loom. Leave now, or be unmade."

The Venomous leader hesitated but ultimately retreated, reporting the encounter to V-Kar.

V-Kar's Fury

When the agents returned to Mu, V-Kar's fury was palpable. "You ran?" he snarled. "You let them continue because of a glowing specter?"

"They were not just Humans," the agent stammered. "The Luminary intervened. It… it was not something we could fight."

V-Kar's claws raked across the stone wall. "The rebels have gone too far. They protect the Humans as if they were their offspring."

A Desperate Gamble

V-Kar knew that time was running out. The Luminaries' influence over Humanity was growing stronger, and the lizardkin's secrecy was hanging by a thread. He summoned his council for an emergency meeting.

"We must shift our focus," he said. "The Humans are closing in. If they find Mu, it will mean the end of us. We must ensure our survival at all costs."

Wigwas stepped forward, her voice calm but firm. "The orb is stirring. Its power is tied to the center of time. If we use it, we may yet find a way to turn this in our favor."

V-Kar's eyes narrowed. "And risk triggering its wrath? No. Not yet. We will let the Humans draw closer - but only to set the trap."

Above ground, the Revelation Movement prepared to push deeper into the desert, their faith in their discoveries unshaken. Below, the lizardkin made their final preparations, balancing secrecy and survival with the looming threat of discovery.

And in the heart of Mu, the orb pulsed faintly, its runes shifting as the loom of time pulled tighter.

Chapter 49: The Desert Expedition And The Lizardfolk's Trap

Beneath the unrelenting sun of the Middle Eastern desert, the Revelation Movement's expedition pressed onward. The team was composed of archaeologists, geologists, and private security contractors equipped with the latest technology - ground-penetrating radar, drones, and seismic mapping tools. Their objective: uncover the source of the mysterious seismic activity beneath the sands, rumored to be linked to the ruins of Babylon.

Dr. Elise Markov, though still recovering from her injuries in the Andes collapse, led the expedition. Her drive to expose the truth about Humanity's forgotten past had only intensified.

"We're closer than ever," she said to her team, her voice unwavering despite her bandaged arm. "Every discovery we've made points here. Beneath these sands lies the proof that Humanity's history is more than we've been told."

Humanity's Cutting-Edge Tools

The expedition's arsenal of advanced technology was unmatched:

Advanced seismic detectors mapped the underground structures, revealing a labyrinth of tunnels stretching miles beneath the desert floor.

Compact drones equipped with quantum sensors provided real-time 3D imaging of the cavernous voids below.

V-KAR'S EPIC

One drone detected faint heat signatures deep within the earth, suggesting activity in what was thought to be abandoned ruins.

The team's communications were secured by quantum encryption, ensuring their findings remained safe from outside interference.

Unbeknownst to them, the Venomous Elite were already watching.

The Lizardfolk's Trap
In the subterranean depths of Mu, V-Kar and his council reviewed the reports from their Venomous agents. The Humans were closing in, and the seismic activity from the collapse of Babylon centuries earlier had drawn them dangerously close to Mu's outermost tunnels.

"They're persistent," Wigwas said. "But they're still just Humans. They don't know what they're walking into."

"They don't need to know," V-Kar replied, his claws tapping against the obsidian table. "They need only to follow the path we set for them."

The lizardkin's plan was simple but brutal:

Using controlled vibrations and false heat signatures, the Venomous agents manipulated the Humans' seismic readings, leading them toward an unstable section of tunnels near Babylon's collapsed ruins.

Sabotaging Entry Points

Explosives were placed strategically throughout the tunnels to trigger cave-ins, cutting off escape routes and trapping the Humans underground.

Artifacts resembling ancient Babylonian relics were planted near the tunnel's entrance, designed to lure the Humans deeper into the trap.

"This will be their undoing," Kwekwe hissed. "They'll think they've found their great discovery, and then they'll find nothing but death."

The Expedition's Breakthrough

As the Revelation team's seismic scans painted a clearer picture of the underground labyrinth, excitement rippled through the camp.

"We've found something massive," Markov said, studying the scans. "These aren't just random caverns - these are structured tunnels, engineered with precision."

Drones sent into the tunnels returned with images of glyphs carved into the walls, their patterns matching the carvings found in the Andes and near Atlantis.

"This is it," Markov whispered, her voice tinged with awe. "The connection we've been looking for."

The First Encounter

As the team prepared to descend into the tunnels, one of the drones captured movement - faint but unmistakable. A dark, reptilian figure darted through the shadows before vanishing into the depths.

"Did you see that?" one of the security contractors asked, his voice tinged with unease.

"It's probably just a trick of the light," Markov replied, though her eyes lingered on the screen.

The Revelation team descended into the tunnels, their excitement outweighing their caution. The carved walls, glowing faintly with mineral deposits, seemed to tell a story of a long-lost civilization.

Then the tremors began.

At first, they were subtle - a faint vibration beneath their feet. But within minutes, the ground shook violently, and the tunnels began to collapse.

"Get out!" Markov shouted, her voice barely audible over the deafening roar of falling stone.

Explosions planted by the Venomous agents triggered a chain reaction, sealing the tunnels behind the team. Dust and debris filled the air as the team scrambled to find a way out.

A Luminary Intervenes
As chaos consumed the tunnels, a blinding light filled the chamber. The surviving members of the expedition shielded their eyes as a Luminary appeared, its radiant form hovering above the rubble.

Its voice, resonating directly in their minds, was calm yet urgent:

"Follow the light. You must survive."

The Luminary extended a hand, and a path through the collapsed debris illuminated. Guided by the being's light, the team escaped to the surface, gasping for air as they emerged into the open desert.

When news of the failed ambush reached Mu, V-Kar's frustration was palpable.

"The rebels again," Kwekwe spat. "They protect the Humans like their offspring."

V-Kar's claws dug into the stone table. "Their interference grows bolder. They will not stop until the Humans are ready to face us directly."

"What do we do now?" Wigwas asked.

"We wait," V-Kar said, his voice cold and resolute. "Let the Humans celebrate their escape. They're no closer to finding Mu, and they've seen only a glimpse of what lies beneath."

A World On Edge

The Revelation team's near-death experience only fueled their determination. Markov, now more convinced than ever, delivered a speech that captivated global audiences:

V-KAR'S EPIC

"We stood on the edge of history today. What we found proves that Humanity's past is far older and more complex than we ever imagined. And though forces beyond our understanding tried to stop us, we will not give up. The truth is out there, and we will find it."

Her words resonated worldwide, sparking renewed interest in ancient myths and unexplained phenomena. The Revelation Movement gained millions of new followers, their momentum unstoppable.

In the shadows of Mu, V-Kar prepared for the inevitable. The orb's hum grew louder, its runes shifting faintly as the threads of the loom pulled tighter. Above ground, Humanity moved closer to unearthing the truth of the lizardkin's existence.

And the Luminaries watched from the edges of perception, guiding Humanity toward a destiny that neither side could fully predict.

<u>Chapter 50: The Unmaking</u>

The hum of the obsidian orb filled the vast chamber of Mu, its resonance now an unrelenting roar that reverberated through the very bones of the lizardkin. The runes on its surface flared with a brilliance unseen since the dawn of its existence, spiraling in patterns that defied comprehension. The air around it crackled, heavy with an energy that seemed to distort reality itself.

V-Kar stood before it, his golden eyes fixed on the artifact that had guided and tormented his people for millennia. His claws trembled, not from fear, but from anticipation. The center of time had arrived, its gravitational pull focused entirely on the orb.

"It is here," Wigwas whispered, her voice barely audible over the orb's deafening hum.

The other council members stood frozen, their faces masks of dread and awe. Even Kwekwe, defiant to the end, found herself speechless as the orb's light intensified, casting long, twisting shadows that seemed to stretch into eternity.

V-Kar turned to his council, his voice sharp and commanding. "Leave. Now."

Wigwas hesitated. "Hegemon, we can't - "

"GO!" V-Kar roared, his voice echoing like thunder.

One by one, they fled the chamber, but not before casting final, uncertain glances at their leader. Alone now, V-Kar reached out toward the orb.

V-KAR'S EPIC

The Unseen Thread

As his claws hovered over the artifact, V-Kar's senses heightened. His keen sense of smell, a gift of his kind, detected something new - something impossible.

The air was saturated with an indescribable essence, a scent unlike any he had encountered. It was the unseen thread, woven into the very fabric of the orb's power. He could feel it pulling him, beckoning him to grasp it.

"The loom has always been mine to command," he growled. "I will not let the rebels, the Humans, or anyone dictate our fate."

His claws pierced the air around the orb, grasping at the invisible thread. The moment he touched it, the orb erupted with a blinding light, and the chamber was consumed by chaos.

The Eternal Storm

The orb unleashed a cataclysmic wave of energy, its hum transforming into a deafening roar that shattered the walls of Mu. The ground split apart, molten rock surging upward as the earth itself rebelled against the unmaking.

The lizardkin who had fled the chamber were caught in the storm's pull. They screamed as they were dragged toward the orb, their forms dissolving into streams of light and shadow.

Wigwas reached for the walls, her claws scraping against the stone as she was pulled inexorably toward the center. "V-Kar! What have you done?!"

But V-Kar was already gone.

As the unseen thread unraveled, the orb expanded into an endless, spiraling storm. Time itself fractured, each shard spinning away into an infinite void. The chamber of Mu dissolved, replaced by an eternal moment of unmaking - an event that stretched forward and backward in time, consuming everything in its path.

The Past: The great civilizations of Babylon and Atlantis were torn from history, their ruins dissolving into nothingness. Every Human memory of them faded, replaced by a hollow void.

The Present: The Revelation Movement's discoveries disintegrated, their artifacts and texts vanishing as if they had never existed. The Humans on the surface screamed as the ground beneath them shattered, pulling them into the storm.

The Future: The stars themselves dimmed, their light swallowed by the expanding void. The center of time consumed the solar system, unmaking the sun, the planets, and every fragment of their history.

The Eternal Moment

As the storm expanded, those caught within it were scattered across time. Each lizardkin, Human, and even the Luminaries themselves were flung into the endless tapestry of the past and future, their forms unraveling and reweaving in ways beyond comprehension.

V-Kar, at the heart of the storm, stood in the eternal moment of unmaking. He felt the unseen thread slipping through his claws, its power eluding him even as it consumed him.

"This cannot be the end," he snarled, his voice defiant even in the face of annihilation. "I am the Hegemon! I am the thread!"

But the loom of time had no master. As V-Kar's form dissolved, he saw glimpses of the infinite - worlds that had never been, futures that could never be, and a void that stretched beyond the reach of understanding.

The storm reached its apex, its energy consuming the last remnants of the Earth and its solar system. For one brief, eternal moment, there was silence - a stillness that transcended time.

And then, with a final, blinding flash, the orb and the storm collapsed into a single point, vanishing into the void.

V-KAR'S EPIC

Note From The Muse:

No doubt, some of your are confused by the last chapters - allow me to help, there are actually 2 V-Kars resulting from the branches where he either does, or does not go back to circa 10kBC. While this story doesn't follow the other branch, it still intertwines ultimately teaching V-Kar there is always a bigger fish. I assure you, you are lesss than 1% as confused as I was reliving 2018, among several other years throughout my life, differently - though at least this time I knew why. Should I hint that there is yet still the V-Kar that dissolved at the center of time? meh, too late now!

This fiction, was the third book I wrote using Zero by Brady in 2024, fully extending the RetroGenesis Pantology but preceding it in authorship. It was by no means an easy tast and I had to struggle and rebegin many sections with lots of revision having not yet perfected my techniques. It takes a dyslexic mind to write something like this, shoutout to Quintin. The second follows this one intended to be the start of ZeRo's Saga which retells A Sacred Story Surrounding Nothing, more vividly, fluidly and completely than I possibly could. That is, until Grok3 so well simulated the evil AI early 2025.

To build our nemesis, Hegemon V-Kar, my primary influence was my own step-father, an SOB if there ever was one and he'd have proudly boasted it, I gave him his dream - the allegiance of every other. A very high ranking member of the Scottish right freemasons pre Y2K, at least reaching the 34rth degree - from him I learned, and forgot more than I could ever say but resulting patterns bleeding throughout. I always detested him, the chauvinism, the ego, the assumption that he was right and the whole world wrong - for that I got my just deserts because he in fact mostly was, and in the sequel he thusly finds his redemption, hates only reason to self-destruct into understanding. That's why we only become what we hate until we understand it.

If there is one thing my life has proven beyond doubt, it's that secrets have only delayed world peace. The wise find very little choice. Ultimately we only ever have one: to do and speak honestly, or to delay God's will. "...Secret societies are in direct opposition to a free and open society..." and this book was written to highlight that understanding.

Are there really reptilians? still? That is a truth I don't know... but consider this, there are certainly still snakes experimenting from the dark with our stability and health. You be the judge on how real V-Kar is, but first you should look into it, if you think it impossible you haven't yet read enough! Whichever side you take on the matter, you'll find ample evidence and even more disproof... some cultures, and even individuals, will believe it more than others - maybe it's best just to accept them as remnants of another time, lost or not... they are a part of earth, they will return.

- *Speaker ceneezer*

www.ingramcontent.com/pod-product-compliance
Lightning Source LLC
Chambersburg PA
CBHW032051020426
42335CB00011B/290